WHEN IT HAPPENED

WHEN IT HAPPENED

A VERY SHORT HISTORY OF
BRITAIN IN DATES, INCLUDING THE
MOST IMPORTANT KINGS & QUEENS,
THE MAJOR BATTLES & OTHER
GREAT EVENTS, TO HELP ANYONE
WHO CANNOT REMEMBER OR
NEVER LEARNED

George Chamier

With illustrations by Charlie Dossett

CONSTABLE · LONDON

Constable & Robinson Ltd
3 The Lanchesters
162 Fulham Palace Road
London W6 9ER
www.constablerobinson.com

This edition published by Constable,
an imprint of Constable & Robinson Ltd, 2006

A copy of the British Library Cataloguing in
Publication Data is available from the British Library

ISBN-13: 978-1-84529-447-2
ISBN-10: 1-84529-447-5

Printed and bound in the EU

For Jan,
without whom this book
would not have been written

Preface

The British history I was taught at school in the 1950s and '60s was full of battles, kings, treaties, Acts and dates. Especially dates. In fact it sometimes seemed that Mr Hartley's history lessons were little more than a memory test of 'when it happened'. Some of them were easy, like the memorable sequence 1215 Magna Carta, 1314 Bannockburn, 1415 Agincourt. Others were tougher, perhaps because the events they were attached to were less vivid (Treaty of Utrecht, anyone?) Sometimes the event itself was vivid enough, like the Black Hole of Calcutta, but the date was hard to locate. So I am certainly not advocating a return to date-bashing as the best way to teach or learn history, but it did give me a basic framework for the past and the ability to get a fix on some important events.

Things are very different now. I recently heard an A-level chief examiner say to his team that they should assume that the students whose work they were marking had started their courses 'from a position of complete ignorance' – in other words, that they had reached the age of sixteen without ever having heard of the Reformation, the Civil War, the American Revolution, the Boer War and so on, let alone knowing the dates attached to these events. University teachers regularly complain that under-graduates now arrive to start their courses with only a 'snapshot' understanding of history, being more or less knowledgeable about the subjects of their A-level course (often 'armband' topics such as Nazi Germany and Communist Russia) but having little or no grasp of the big picture. In order to pin the tail on the donkey, you need to have a rough idea of the shape of the animal.

This book is about the important dates in British history only – not because I subscribe to the patriotic *Our Island Story* way of thinking, but because you have to start somewhere, and where better than with the history of your own country? Plenty of time to move on when the history bug bites you and you want to find out more. The events chosen are intended to give an overview, and though obviously there isn't space to go into detailed consequences, I've tried to give pointers.

Professional historians study the rise and fall of empires, kingdoms, governments, political and social movements. They look at the long- and short-term causes of crisis, conflict and stability. But even the professionals cannot get away from the fact that when it comes to the crunch, history is the record of 'One Damned Thing After Another'. History is a story, and if you don't know the sequence of events you cannot make sense of it.

55 BC

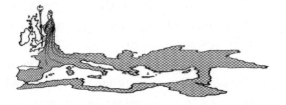

Julius Caesar's Invasion of Britain

Not only the first memorable date in British history, it is also the first accurate one because prior to that our ancestors had not recorded events by year. Although outside their empire, Britain was well known to the Romans as an exporter of tin (from Cornwall), as well as slaves, hides and good hunting dogs. There were only a few towns, but farming, fortifications and metalwork were all well developed and the country was divided into lots of small tribal kingdoms.

Julius Caesar boasted 'Veni, Vidi, Vici' ('I came, I saw, I conquered'), but this did not apply to Britain: although he came and saw, he conquered only for a bit then went away. He came back again a year later with 800 ships, legions and cavalry support. Roman military discipline proved too much for the Britons despite the fearsome effect of the British war chariots. Some British tribes surrendered, others collaborated, and Caesar eventually gained control of most of the south-east. He took hostages, fixed an annual tribute to be paid by the Britons and then sailed back to the Continent.

Caesar's invasion was not the result of deliberate policy but more a bid for power on his part back home. He led an army which had conquered Gaul (modern France), but with Gaul subdued he risked losing his military command. Further conquests would achieve glory for his name, impress public opinion back in Rome and provide plunder to swell his war chest.

49 BC Caesar became dictator of Rome and was assassinated five years later, in 44 BC, on the Ides of March.

27 BC Octavian declared 'Augustus' (revered one) and became first Roman Emperor.

AD 37 Caligula became Emperor. Mad as hatter, he is remembered for appointing his favourite horse as a consul and for sleeping with his sister. He also decided to invade Britain and assembled troops on the Channel shore in preparation – but then ordered them to collect sea shells which he sent back to Rome as plunder of war. Not surprisingly, he was soon assassinated by the palace guard. He was replaced by his uncle Claudius, who had a club foot, a stammer and a somewhat shaky hold on power.

AD 43

The Roman Occupation

Claudius decided that he needed a great military victory and the appearance of a British warlord called Caractacus encouraged him to invade. An army of 40,000 crossed the Channel and were victorious in a series of tough battles. Claudius arrived in person to direct the final stages of the campaign before returning to Rome to celebrate his triumph.

Within three years Rome had established a military capital at Camulodunum (Colchester), was in control of south and east Britain, and had started to penetrate the north and west as well. Londinium (London) was founded three years later: a small settlement already existed, but the Romans created a town, military garrison and centre for trade. Caractacus, leader of anti-Roman resistance in Britain, was captured in AD 51 and taken to Rome, where he was put on show as evidence of Claudius's triumph in Britain. In recognition of his bravery, he was then released and lived out the rest of his life in Rome.

Boudicca's Rebellion

A mixture of Roman insensitivity and British resentment boiled over in a rebellion which had the Romans running scared. On the death of the king of the Iceni tribe (who lived in what is now Norfolk and part of Suffolk) the Romans grabbed his land and abused his widow Boudicca and her daughters. The neighbouring Trinovantes tribe (who lived in what is now another part of Suffolk and Essex) were already upset by the stationing of Roman soldiers in their territory and joined Boudicca in what became a widespread revolt.

The legendary picture of Boudicca as an Amazonian warrior queen riding into battle in a chariot with her hair streaming in the wind is just that – a legend. There is no evidence that she personally fought in battle. But she must have been an intensely charismatic leader because she put together an immense army (200,000 according to some accounts), which defeated a Roman legion and sacked Colchester, London and St Albans before being massacred by the main forces of the

Roman governor. Boudicca herself survived the battle but is said to have taken poison shortly afterwards rather than fall into Roman hands again.

77 The Romans completed their conquest of Wales, including Anglesey, which was a stronghold of the Druids, the priests of the ancient British religion.

83 Battle of Mons Graupius. The Governor Agricola led an army north into Caledonia (now called Scotland). He marched through the south-west, but the main thrust was up the east coast with a naval force in support. The legions finally faced the Caledonian tribesmen in a pitched battle at Mons Graupius. The exact site has never been identified, but it is probably somewhere in modern Aberdeenshire and it gave its name to the Grampian mountains. The Roman historian Tacitus put stirring words into the mouth of the Caledonian chieftain Calgacus, who declared 'we Caledonians have never been slaves' and described Roman rule with the chilling words 'they make a desert and call it peace'. But the Roman victory was over-whelming and although it did not lead to permanent settlement of Caledonia, the army left garrisons in strategic sites to keep the tribes in check.

Hadrian's Wall

Pressure on the Roman Empire's other frontiers led to the withdrawal of some troops from Britain and the decision to stop expanding to the north. The Emperor Hadrian visited in AD 122 and ordered the construction of a fortified stone wall from the Solway to the Tyne. To the north, apart from occasional raids to show the Caledonians who was boss, Rome decided to leave the tribes to their own devices for the time being.

South of the Wall, the province of Britannia was Romanized: towns grew in size and acquired civilized features such as public baths, a forum, temples and theatres; a network of long straight roads was built; Roman law, taxation and bureaucracy took root; the local British upper classes were absorbed into Roman society and their sons were educated in Roman ways; Britons were recruited into the legions; many Britons became Roman citizens; the Latin language was commonly spoken; and Roman dress was adopted. Roman villas, big country houses at the centre of large landed estates, became a feature of the British country-side. Of course, the Romanization was not total: Britain was, after all, a distant frontier province when seen from Rome – 'provincial' probably describes it pretty accurately – and the island's climate as well as its relative poverty prevented the complete adoption of a civilized Roman way of life as lived in Italy and the Mediterranean. The British language survived alongside Latin, as did local religious beliefs, and residents of more remote areas probably lived lives which were hardly changed by Roman rule.

It is a myth to think of the Britons as sullen and downtrodden subjects during the centuries of Roman occupation. Many of them actively cooperated with Roman rule, most benefited from it in a material way, and when the Roman empire started to fall apart in the fourth and fifth centuries, the Romano-British, as they should be called, did their best to keep Roman culture and government going.

138 Building of the Antonine Wall (between the rivers Clyde and Forth in central Scotland). It was abandoned in 163.

212 The Emperor Caracalla granted Roman citizenship to all free inhabitants of the Empire and as a result many Britons become 'Romans'.

275 Shore forts were constructed in the south-east to protect Britain against Saxon invaders.

293 The Emperor Diocletian divided the Roman Empire into two, each part with its own ruler and deputy. Britannia was split into four provinces.

303 Diocletian started a general persecution of Christians throughout the empire.

304 St Alban became the first Christian martyr in Britain.

306

Constantine the Great Proclaimed Emperor at York

The third century was not a happy one for most of the Roman Empire. There was a succession of short-lived emperors, usually made and unmade by the army; the coinage virtually collapsed; and barbarian tribes constantly pressed on the frontiers.

Britain had escaped many of these troubles, although rival emperors twice emerged here, the tribes known as Picts and Scots began to attack from the north and west across Hadrian's Wall, and the first Saxon raiders attacked south-eastern coasts.

Under the new system instituted by the Emperor Diocletian to deal with the anarchy, Constantius was the ruler of the empire's western half. While campaigning in Britain, he died at York and his son Constantine was proclaimed emperor there by his legions. A long series of wars against his rivals ended in 324 with Constantine in command of the whole empire. He kept an interest in Britain, visiting at least once and ordering major building work at York, but his most important legacy was his conversion to Christianity, which caused him to proclaim toleration for the church and to promote it throughout the empire. Britain was no exception, and by 315 there were at least three British bishoprics, including London.

367 'The Conspiracy of the Barbarians', so called because in this year Britain suffered simultaneous attacks by Picts, Scots and Saxons (although there is no evidence that these were deliberately concerted).

378 The Battle of Hadrianople at which the Emperor Valens was defeated and killed by the Goths. This was a substantial nail in the coffin of the Western Roman Empire.

383 Magnus Maximus proclaimed emperor by his troops in Britain. Known in Britain as Macsen Wledig, he was in fact a Spaniard though this did not stop him rapidly conquering Gaul, Spain and Italy before being defeated and executed by the legitimate emperor, Theodosius. Maximus's campaigns had the effect of draining Britain of troops.

397 The Roman general Stilicho campaigned in Britain against the Picts, Scots and Saxons. He transferred command of many units from Roman officers to local British chieftains.

406 Barbarian hordes (Suevi, Vandals, Alans, Burgundians) crossed the frozen Rhine into Roman Gaul. Britain was now cut off from contact with Rome.

407 Constantine III was proclaimed emperor in Britain and withdrew troops from Britain to march on Italy.

410 The Sack of Rome by the Goths under their leader Alaric.

410

The Romans Leave Britain

This is the traditional date given for the end of Roman Britain, but we should not imagine the final shipload of legionaries waving goodbye to their British girlfriends and the island immediately reverting to pre-Roman tribalism. It was not as simple as that.

The empire was certainly in crisis, with barbarian armies pouring across the frontiers, rival emperors slugging it out and Rome's resources stretched to the limit. Britain's island status had always made it a secure reservoir of men and supplies for the armies attempting to defend the continental provinces. Apart from that, hanging on to the remote British provinces was unlikely to have been a high priority for Rome, and all the legions had probably already gone by 410. But after three-and-a-half centuries as part of the empire the Britons were as much Roman as British, and the departure of the last legion did not mark a sharp break with the past. Roman buildings and towns remained; literacy and Christianity had taken hold under Roman rule; and Roman culture and technology were still valued.

In the two centuries after the collapse of Roman Britain, invaders from continental Europe arrived in large numbers – Angles, Saxons and Jutes from what is now northern Germany and Denmark. One of these peoples, the Angles eventually gave their name to England ('Angle-land'). These were the darkest of dark ages and our knowledge of events is very sketchy, but we should imagine a period of semi-continuous warfare during which the invaders gradually displaced the local British rulers and drove the native Britons westwards. Some Britons left for north-western Gaul, in the process giving their name to what is now Brittany. A typically terse entry from the *Anglo-Saxon Chronicle* reads: '514 In this year the West Saxons, Stuf and Wihtgar, came with three ships . . . and fought with the Britons and put them to flight'.

428 Vortigern and the Saxons. With the fifth century, Britain entered its Dark Age, a period in which historical sources are dubious, dates are often uncertain and characters shadowy. There probably was a British warlord called Vortigern ('great leader') and it was probably around this time that he recruited Saxon mercenaries, the legendary Hengist and Horsa, to help defend Britain. They then turned on their British allies, thus opening the door to Britain for the Anglo-Saxon invaders who arrived here in large numbers and eventually seized control of the country.

446 The final British appeal for help was refused
by Aetius (the 'last of the Romans'), Roman governor
of Gaul. He had his hands full dealing with Attila the
Hun (known to the Romans as 'the scourge of God').

**448 Large numbers of Saxon invaders landed in
southern Britain**, as recorded by Bede, the Northumbrian monk whose *Ecclesiastical History of the English
People* (731) is the single greatest source for early
English history.

452 The Huns invaded Italy.

476 The End of the Western Roman Empire. The
Emperor Romulus Augustulus was deposed by the
Gothic leader Odoacer, who refused the now-meaning-
less title of emperor and called himself 'King of Italy'.

496 Battle of Mount Badon. This is a dubious date
but it brings into the picture the greatest of all British
mythical figures – Arthur. Most people have a mental
picture of King Arthur's world which includes knights
in armour; jousting; maidens in distress; a round table;
the Holy Grail; Merlin, Guinevere and Lancelot; the
sword in the stone; and the king who will return when
Britain needs him. It is impossible to discover from
the historical sources whether King Arthur actually
existed or what he achieved. All we can say is that *if*
Arthur existed, he was *probably* a Romano-British war
leader attempting to defend Britain against the invading

Saxons and that he *may* have defeated them at a battle at an unidentified place called Mount Badon at this time.

563 St Columba founded a monastery on the Island of Iona, coming from Ireland, which had already been converted in the previous century by St Patrick. From Iona, Christianity spread throughout Scotland.

597

St Augustine Arrives in Canterbury

Pope Gregory the Great, so the story goes, met some blond young slaves from England in Rome and on being told that they were Angles, he declared 'not Angles but angels' and despatched Augustine to convert their pagan fellows at home. Augustine's mission arrived in Kent, the richest and most powerful of the Anglo-Saxon kingdoms, and succeeded in converting its king, Aethelbert, who granted him the land on which to build the first cathedral at Canterbury. Conversion of the other Anglo-Saxon kingdoms was a slow process, but Christianity had been replanted in England and contact with Rome restored.

St Augustine may have succeeded in converting some of the English to Christianity, but this does not mean that Britain was a peaceful place in the next couple of centuries. In fact, British history becomes a confused chronicle of battle, murder, betrayal, pillage, plague and famine. In these anarchic years Britons, Saxons,

Picts and Scots fought each other in a shifting pattern of alliances, and about all we can say for certain is that the Anglo–Saxon kingdoms gradually gained control of most of England.

664 The Synod of Whitby was a gathering of bishops of the church at which the date for Easter was debated between followers of the Roman church (who came over with St Augustine) and followers of the Celtic church (who came over with St Columba). The Roman church won the argument and this was the beginning of the end for an independent Celtic church. Britain came under the religious authority of Rome, where it stayed until Henry VIII's reign.

685 The battle of Nechtansmere. The Picts defeated a Northumbrian invasion, thus ensuring that most of Scotland would never come under Anglo–Saxon rule.

700 The Lindisfarne Gospels, a beautifully decorated manuscript, was copied and illustrated by the monk Eadfrith.

784 Offa's Dyke built. Offa, King of Mercia, ordered the construction of a fortified ditch (Offa's Dyke) along the Welsh border, marking a permanent division between Anglo–Saxon England and Celtic Wales.

793

The Vikings Attack Lindisfarne

'In this year the ravaging of heathen men destroyed God's church at Lindisfarne with brutal robbery and slaughter,' said the *Anglo-Saxon Chronicle*. As if life in Britain was not precarious enough, the next two hundred years saw the age of the Vikings: terrifying Scandinavian pirates such as Eric Bloodaxe and Thorfinn Skull-Splitter who came to plunder the weak, trade with the strong and eventually settle, carving out kingdoms and blending their genes and language into the British mix.

The Vikings came from Norway and Denmark. The former specialized in attacking and invading north-west England, Ireland and Scotland – in fact the Orkney and Shetland Islands remained part of Norway until the fifteenth century and Shetlanders spoke a Norse language until the 1800s.

The Danes concentrated on England and created kingdoms for themselves in the south and north-east, East Anglia and the Midlands. The invaders were only ever a minority of the population, but they left their mark on the English language (words like 'sky', 'sister', 'bairn') and on many place-names – such as those ending in -by, -thorpe and -thwaite.

828 King Egbert of Wessex was recognized as overlord by other English kings. Wessex, with its capital at Winchester, was the main Anglo-Saxon centre holding out against the Danes.

843 Kenneth MacAlpin, King of the Scots, defeated the Picts and claimed to rule over the whole of Scotland.

865 The Great Heathen Army of Vikings landed in England led by Halfdan and Ivar the Boneless, sons of Ragnar Hairybreeks.

878

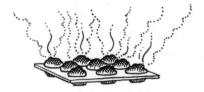

King Alfred Beats the Danes

Only one English monarch is known as 'Great'. King Alfred of Wessex earned this title by uniting the Anglo-Saxons against the invaders, defeating the Great Heathen Army and making a lasting peace treaty with them at Wedmore. However, all this did not come easy. At one point Alfred's fortunes had sunk so low that he and a band of followers were hiding from the Vikings in the Somerset marshes; an old woman scolded the king, travelling in disguise, for allowing her cakes to burn while he brooded on the fate of his kingdom. Alfred showed his good and kindly nature by apologizing.

As well as being a successful soldier, Alfred was a scholar and a visionary: he built schools and monasteries, translated Latin texts and deliberately used English as the language of education, thus instilling in his people the beginnings of a sense of national identity. Above all, he brought peace: the Danes retreated to the area known as the Danelaw (East Anglia, the east Midlands and the north) and the rest of England gradually came under the control of the kings of Wessex.

937 King Athelstan of Wessex claimed the title 'King of all Britain' when he defeated an alliance of Scots and Vikings at the battle of Brunanburh.

1016 The Vikings returned in force at the turn of the millennium. Unfortunately for the English, their throne was occupied at the time by Aethelred the Unready. His technique for dealing with the Danes was to buy them off with protection money (danegeld), but of course this only encouraged them to come back. The Viking leader, Swein Forkbeard, seized the throne and, when Aethelred died in 1016, Swein's son Cnut killed Aethelred's son and then married his widowed mother, Emma of Normandy. Cnut also gained control of Denmark and Norway, and England became part of a Scandinavian empire. Cnut himself was evidently a man of intelligence and humour: when his sycophantic courtiers suggested that even the tide would obey him, he sat on the beach and deliberately allowed the waves to lap over his feet. Cnut's sons died without heirs and the English throne passed to Edward, son of Aethelred the Unready, who had been brought up in Normandy, was deeply interested in religion and who had taken a vow of chastity as a young man.

1066

The Norman Conquest

This is the most famous date in British history – and a year which packed in plenty of drama. King Edward died childless (not surprisingly in view of the chastity), and as a result Harold, Earl of Wessex, grabbed the throne. He had to deal with two rival claimants: Harald Hardrada, King of Norway, and William, Duke of Normandy. Hardrada invaded first, sailing up the Humber and defeating the English army sent to face him. This was Harold's finest hour: he marched his army north for four days, took the invaders by surprise and destroyed them in battle at Stamford Bridge, near York. Unfortunately, he had left the south unguarded, and just three days later William of Normandy's warships landed at Pevensey. Harold's elated but exhausted army turned round and marched south to confront this new threat. The two armies came face to face at Hastings. On the Norman side were professional soldiers, many of them armoured knights on horseback. The larger English army consisted of the house-carles (bodyguard) of Harold and his allies, some other professional soldiers and a mass of peasants armed with pitchforks and slingshots.

At first the Normans were unable to pierce the massed ranks of the English infantry. But when Harold's men broke ranks to chase the Normans they thought were retreating it was a fatal blunder. The Norman cavalry turned round and rode in among the English, hacking them down. Harold was killed by an arrow in the eye, the battle was lost and William earned himself the title 'Conqueror'. He marched to London and was crowned king in Westminster Abbey on Christmas Day.

1067 William started building the Tower of London, the great fortress which demonstrated his power and dominated the city of London.

1086

Domesday Book

There was resistance to Norman rule in various parts of England – most seriously in the north, where it was encouraged by the Scots and the Danes. In the campaign known as 'the Harrying of the North', William devastated rebel areas, slaughtering livestock, burning farms and executing prisoners. The last Englishman to resist the Conquest was Hereward the Wake, who held out for a few years with a forlorn band in the Fens.

Now England was all William's and he set about dividing it up amongst his followers. The record of this carve-up can be seen in the Domesday Book, the great survey of the land and who owned it. Published twenty years after the Conquest, it records that just four members of the old English nobility were still in possession of their lands; all the rest had been evicted in favour of Norman barons. Not just a new king, but an entire new ruling class had taken over England. They also owned land on the Continent and spoke French – indeed, their whole culture was French.

1087 William the Conqueror died. Normandy went to his eldest son Robert, and England to his second son William, who became William II, but was known as William Rufus because of his red hair.

1100 William Rufus was killed hunting in the New Forest. The man who fired the arrow, Walter Tirel, fled the country, and William's brother, Henry, who was also in the hunting party, seized the royal treasure and hurried to London, where he was crowned just three days later. Whether or not Rufus was murdered, his death was convenient to say the least for young Henry. Henry I ruled England for the next thirty-five years. No less ruthless than his father, he was more calculating and better educated (he was known as 'Beauclerk' meaning 'fine scholar').

1120 The wreck of the White Ship. William, the only legitimate son and heir of Henry I, was drowned in the Channel. The two rival candidates for succession to the throne of England were Henry's daughter, Matilda, and his nephew, Stephen, and the result of their conflict was disastrous.

1135

Stephen and Matilda's Civil War

A monk writing his chronicle described the state of England between 1135 and 1154 as the time when 'Christ and his angels slept'. When Henry I died, his nephew Stephen was quick to seize the throne. Henry I's daughter, Matilda, had a better claim, but she was in France when her father died and the English barons disliked the idea of a female ruler. She soon returned to England, however, to make good her claim, and had some powerful allies, especially King David of Scotland, who grabbed the chance to invade England and add a slice of the north to his kingdom. Almost twenty years of civil war between Matilda and Stephen followed. At one point Stephen was taken prisoner and Matilda proclaimed herself queen, but she taxed the citizens of London so harshly that they rejected her and she was eventually forced to flee to France. It was a period of anarchy and misery for England: government broke down and powerful barons became local warlords, many of them changing sides as it suited them; the church's property was plundered; and ordinary folk suffered robbery and rape at the hands of both sides' armies of mercenaries.

1154 Stephen died and Matilda's son succeeded to the throne as Henry II. He possessed not just England but also more than half of France, through inheritance from his father and his marriage to Eleanor of Aquitaine. He was the most powerful ruler in Europe, and England was just part of the Angevin (from Anjou, Henry's father's land) empire. In the same year, Nicholas Breakspear became the only English pope (as Adrian IV). All in all, it was a good year for England.

1170

Murder of Thomas Becket*

In Henry's early years as king, Thomas Becket was not only his Chancellor but also his friend and companion, hunting, feasting and jousting with him. But then Henry made him Archbishop of Canterbury and Becket devoted himself to the church rather than to the king, and the two men fell out. Becket refused to allow priests to be tried in the ordinary courts and excommunicated bishops who took the king's side in the dispute. This was an insult Henry could not ignore, and one night at dinner he uttered the fateful question, 'Who will rid me of this turbulent priest?' Four loyal knights took the king at his word and rode to Canterbury, where they found Becket at prayer in the cathedral. They butchered him in front of the altar.

Henry was devastated by what he had had done to his old friend and as a penance he walked barefoot through Canterbury while eighty monks whipped him. Despite the murder of Becket, Henry II ruled for thirty-five years, during which he recovered the north from Scottish control, invaded and claimed overlordship of Ireland, and restored the rule of law and stable government to England.

Beckett was canonized only two years after his murder, and the shrine of St Thomas at Canterbury became one of the wealthiest and most famous in Europe. It was a popular destination for pilgrims, including the characters described in Chaucer's *Canterbury Tales* (see 1387).

*Thomas Becket is generally preferred to the alternative spelling Thomas à Becket.

1190

Richard the Lionheart Goes on Crusade

Richard Coeur de Lion (Lionheart) was an A-list European celebrity in his day. He was also undoubtedly brave and a great warrior, but not much use as king of England. He was brought up in France, had scarcely been to England before he became king, probably could not speak English and spent just ten months of his ten-year reign in the country. He was so keen to raise troops to go on crusade to the Holy Land that he is reported to have said, 'If I could find a buyer I would sell London itself'. He was not a particularly pleasant character: he rebelled against his own father in Henry II's last years and took revenge on anyone who crossed him. What gained him everlasting fame was his achievements as a crusader: he captured the cities of Acre and Jaffa, defeated the great Muslim commander Saladin and then made an advantageous peace treaty with him. However, on his way home Richard was captured in Austria and an enormous ransom had to be paid by his

English subjects to free him. Legend has it that he was discovered in captivity when he responded from his cell to the song of the minstrel Blondel; some say – rather surprisingly for such an apparently butch king – that Blondel was also his lover. It may have been during Richard's reign that the legend of Robin Hood arose. Historians have spent a lot of time searching for the original Robin Hood, and many would place him at a later date. But the most popular version (as memorably portrayed by Errol Flynn in the 1938 film) has Robin as the defender of the liberties of loyal Englishmen oppressed by the harsh rule of Prince John while their king is abroad on crusade.

1215

Magna Carta

King John has gone down in history as the classic 'bad king'. He was a poor leader in peace and war, greedy, untrustworthy and cruel (he once had the wife and children of an enemy starved to death). His nicknames – 'Softsword' and 'Lackland' – speak for themselves, but he was not a complete failure: he was an intelligent, educated man and had considerable success in some of his military campaigns, especially against the Irish, Welsh and Scots. But what doomed his reputation was the loss of most of his lands in France to the French king. He taxed England heavily to raise armies to recover these lands, but failed to do so, finally being defeated at the battle of Bouvines (1214). This was the final straw for the English barons, who had already lost their own French lands as a result of John's military failures and been oppressed by his tyrannical rule. They forced him to meet them at Runnymede on the Thames near Windsor, where the most famous document in English history was drawn up and signed.

Magna Carta is often thought of as some sort of guarantee of liberty for all men, the beginning of the road to democracy and universal human rights. It was nothing of the sort. The barons were not interested in the common man, they just wanted their own positions preserved, and most of Magna Carta is to do with limiting the king's powers and making sure he observed the rights and privileges of the nobility. But it does put forward the important idea (which not all later kings obeyed) that the king should be under the law; and it does lay down some fundamental principles which stand for all time, such as: 'No free man shall be taken, imprisoned, dispossessed, outlawed or exiled or in any way ruined . . . except by the lawful judgement of his equals or by the law of the land'.

True to form, King John signed Magna Carta but within weeks turned on the barons and started to make war on them. At first he was successful but then things began to go wrong: on campaign in Lincolnshire all his household belongings disappeared in the quicksands of the Wash, and he died from dysentery after gorging on cider and peaches.

1265

Simon de Montfort and the First Parliament

Bad King John was succeeded by his nine-year-old son, who became Henry III. Although he reigned for over fifty years, Henry was not a great success either: he failed to regain his father's lands in France, appointed a string of unpopular French and Italian favourites to top jobs in church and government, and ignored the limits on royal power which had been laid down in Magna Carta. Not surprisingly, the barons were unhappy with his rule, and they forced him to sign a deal (the Provisions of Oxford) in 1258 that made him agree to take the advice of a council of fifteen noblemen. Henry then went back on his word. His brother-in-law, Simon de Montfort, described as the 'shield and defender of the kingdom', led the opposition to the king. De Montfort's father had been a ruthless persecutor of the Cathar heretics in France, but the son seems to have been genuinely motivated by the interests of England and the English people. A brilliant general, he defeated the king's army at the battle of Lewes and assembled a parliament (from the French *parler*, to talk) to discuss a settlement. This was not the first ever parliament, but it was the first representative one, because members came from both the counties and the towns.

De Montfort did not get the chance to show what he could do because he was defeated and killed within the year by Prince Edward (later Edward I) at the battle of Evesham. But it was a start towards representative government.

1284

The First Prince of Wales

Henry III's son, King Edward I, was a big man in every way – 'so tall of build', a contemporary wrote, 'that he was head and shoulders above ordinary men' and was known as Longshanks. He was a great soldier and known as 'the hammer of the Scots', although the first target of his armies was Wales.

The kings of England already claimed they were overlords of Wales but they left much of the country under the control of native Welsh princes. Prince Llewelyn led a rebellion against Edward and, despite the effectiveness of their longbows (which would be adopted by the English as their key weapon in years to come), the Welsh rebels were soundly defeated. By the Statute of Wales (1284) Edward officially made the country part of his kingdom and appointed his son (the future Edward II) Prince of Wales, the title which has been used ever since by heirs to the throne. To maintain control of the country Edward built a magnificent series of castles, including Caernarvon and Harlech, which are his greatest memorials.

Edward planned to unite Scotland with England by marrying his son to the 'Maid of Norway', the three-year-old heir to the Scottish throne. Unfortunately, the little girl did not survive the journey from Norway, but Edward was given another chance when the Scots nobles asked him to choose between the possible candidates for the throne. He chose John Balliol, who he believed he could keep under his thumb, but Edward's high-handed attitude provoked the Scots to ally themselves with France (the 'auld alliance', which lasted for most of the next three hundred years) and take up arms against him. Edward's response was devastating: he invaded Scotland in 1296, took the throne for himself and removed the Stone of Destiny from Scone, where Scots kings were crowned, and placed it in Westminster Abbey (it was stolen by Scottish nationalists in the 1950s and finally returned to Scotland in 1996). The Scots did not take this treatment lying down, and Edward had to campaign in Scotland almost every year for the rest of his reign. The high point of Scottish resistance came with the leadership of William Wallace (portrayed rather unrealistically by Mel Gibson in *Braveheart*), until he was betrayed to the enemy and taken as a prisoner to London, where he was subjected to a rebel's death – dragged for four miles behind a horse to Smithfield, before being drawn and quartered.

1314

Battle of Bannockburn

As in football, so in war, the Scots usually lose to the English, but this means that they cherish their victories all the more. No victory was greater than Bannockburn. After Wallace's death, Robert the Bruce became the leader of Scottish resistance. To begin with he had to flee from the English, during which time he was inspired while hiding in a cave by the sight of a spider spinning its web to 'try, try and try again'. He was also ruthless enough to murder his main rival, the Red Comyn. Luckily for Bruce he was faced not by the remorseless Edward I but by Edward II, who could never live up to his father.

Young Edward foolishly allowed the Scots time to build up their forces, and when he finally confronted them at Bannockburn, the English cavalry, without enough support from archers, was broken on the spearpoints of the Scots infantry. It was a crushing victory, which showed the Scots that English armies were not invincible. The battle was followed by Scottish raids across the border which caused panic even in the south of England. Bannockburn was the battle which in effect ended any chance that the kings of England would add Scotland to their empire.

1320 The Declaration of Arbroath: 'For as long as there shall but one hundred of us be left alive we will never give consent to subject ourselves to the dominion of the English'. This was Scotland's declaration of independence which was sent to the Pope asking for recognition of Scotland as an independent nation.

1327 The murder of Edward II: the classic 'weak king', Edward was bored to tears by the business of government and much happier amusing himself with a succession of handsome young men like Piers Gaveston. His queen, Isabella, and her lover Roger de Mortimer schemed to depose him and had the unfortunate Edward murdered at Berkeley Castle, reputedly by means of a red-hot poker stuck up a very painful place.

1328 The Treaty of Edinburgh. England acknowledged Robert Bruce as King of Scotland, confirming Scotland's independence.

1337–1453

The Hundred Years' War

This was not a hundred (or even 116 if you count) years of continuous fighting, but a state of war which from time to time escalated into full-scale campaigns and sometimes stopped for periods of truce.

The main cause of the war was the ancestral claim of the kings of England to the throne of France, and the best way to make sense of the complicated ebb and flow of events is to think of the war as having four phases.

Phase One (1337–60) saw England enjoying success in battle (Crécy and Poitiers) and gaining land in France. In Phase Two (1360–1413) there were periods of peace but England, despite carrying out raids, lost most of its gains and the English coast came under attack from French fleets. In Phase Three (1413–31) England was successful again as Henry V invaded and won the battle of Agincourt; by 1430 England controlled more of France than at any other time in the war, and in 1431 the young Henry VI was actually crowned King of France in Paris. But it couldn't last.

Phase Four (1431–53) saw the French, inspired initially by Joan of Arc, force the English out of all of France except for Calais.

In addition to the set-piece battles were many sieges and *chevauchées*, which were expeditions by bands of English soldiers aimed at destruction and plunder; there were also invasion scares in England – the French actually captured the Isle of Wight for a brief period, and France's allies the Scots raided across the border. The war was fought with savagery at times – more than 3,000 men, women and children were killed in cold blood at the siege of Limoges – but the rules of chivalric warfare were also obeyed, at least between the knights on either side: an enemy who surrendered was treated with hospitality, not least because he could be ransomed for a large sum. The armies of both sides were led by mounted knights in armour. The French had a fixed belief in the superiority of cavalry and the cavalry charge, while the English were prepared to be more flexible in their tactics. The English longbow fired faster and had a longer range than the crossbow used by the French, but in the later stages of the war the French made better use of the emerging technology of gunpowder.

1346

Battle of Crécy

Edward III invaded Normandy and led his army across northern France. The enemy caught up with them at Crécy, where the French cavalry, over-confident of its superiority, attacked without a proper plan, charging uphill over muddy ground which slowed the men down and made them sitting ducks for the Welsh long-bowmen of Edward's army. Their arrows were able to pierce the knights' armour and a chronicler wrote 'they let fly their arrows so wholly together that it seemed snow'. This was the battle in which Edward's son the Black Prince won his spurs. Edward followed up the victory by besieging Calais. Six citizens of the town offered him their lives if he would spare the town, and he accepted his queen's plea to be merciful to them and the town itself. It became a valuable base which was to remain in the possession of England for two centuries.

1348

The Black Death

In a period of about two years something like a third to half of the population of the British Isles was killed by bubonic or pneumonic plague. The plague killed its victims quickly – few lasted more than a week. The effects of death on this scale were enormous. The living were unable to bury the dead except in mass graves; whole villages were deserted; so-called flagellants saw the plague as God's punishment for sin and paraded in public whipping themselves; others thought the end of the world was coming and seized the opportunity to indulge in orgies of drink and sex. Nobody understood how plague spread (in fact it spread from rats to humans by flea bites) and the only way people could avoid it was to flee. This was hopeless when the entire British mainland was affected. The plague returned after its first assault – there were six more major outbreaks before 1400. Economically, the Black Death was bad news for landowners and employers, who were faced with a shortage of labour and consequently high wage demands, but good news for employees and tenants because unoccupied land was now available.

1349 The Order of the Garter. While the Countess of Salisbury, who was probably the king's mistress, was dancing at court her garter fell to the floor. Hearing the sniggers of those around him, Edward III picked it up, declaring 'honi soit qui mal y pense'('evil to him who thinks evil'). This became the motto of the order of knighthood founded in memory of the incident. The order still exists today and members are appointed personally by the monarch.

1351 The Statute of Labourers made it illegal for employers to pay wages above the level offered in 1346, when the Black Death started.

1356 Battle of Poitiers. Once again, the French underestimated the power of the longbow and charged an English defensive position only to be massacred. The French king and 2,000 of his men, including many nobles, were taken prisoner and ransomed: the price for the king alone was three million gold crowns.

1381

The Peasants' Revolt

The Peasants' Revolt was an attack on the power of the aristocracy and was triggered by a series of protests against the Poll Tax, which had been introduced to pay for the Hundred Years' War. Marching from Kent and Essex and led by Wat Tyler, Jack Straw and the priest John Ball, as many as 100,000 people converged on London, where they destroyed tax records, looted and burned buildings and killed the Archbishop of Canterbury and the Treasurer. However, the young King Richard II (he was only fourteen) courageously met the rebels at Smithfield. They believed his promise to give in to their demands. He was even able to talk them round after Wat Tyler had been killed by the Lord Mayor of London. But of course he was lying. As soon as the peasants dispersed he had their leaders arrested and hanged.

1387

Chaucer begins
The Canterbury Tales

Geoffrey Chaucer had a varied career as a soldier, diplomat and administrator, and it was around this date that he began work on his masterpiece: *The Canterbury Tales*. It is an unfinished poem of 17,000 lines about a group of pilgrims who set out from London to travel to the shrine of St Thomas Becket in Canterbury. The different pilgrims – including the knight, the pardoner and the wife of Bath – each tell a story along the way. They are not only memorable as individuals but also a superb cross-section of English society at the time. Some of the tales have an obvious moral, some are funny and others bawdy. Chaucer chose to write in English – not in Latin, which was the usual language for literary works, nor in Norman French, which was the language of the aristocracy, government and the law. English was the language of ordinary people and the street, and as a result Chaucer can justifiably be called the father of English literature.

1390 Wycliffe's Bible. John Wycliffe, an Oxford don, produced a version of the Bible in English. He and his followers, known as the Lollards (from the Dutch 'to mumble' because of their devotion to reading and prayer), attacked the wealth of the church, denied the need for priests and questioned official teaching on Holy Communion. Not surprisingly, they were persecuted under a law called *De heretico comburendo* or 'Why heretics should be burned'.

1397 Dick Whittington became Lord Mayor of London.

1399

Murder of Richard II

In the later years of his reign Richard II ruled ruthlessly, arresting leading nobles on charges of conspiracy, banishing them and seizing their land. Among those he banished was Henry Bolingbroke, son of John of Gaunt and Blanche of Lancaster, and grandson of Edward III – a man with a pretty good claim to the throne himself. When Gaunt died, Richard confiscated the family lands and increased Henry's sentence to exile for life. Henry defied him and returned to England with just forty followers. Richard was away in Ireland but dislike of him was so widespread that Henry soon had an army of thousands. He got Parliament to formally depose his cousin Richard, then imprisoned him in Pontefract Castle, had him murdered and took the title Henry IV. His reign was troubled by rebellions and illness – he is the king for whom Shakespeare coined the phrase 'uneasy lies the head that wears a crown' – and his seizure of the throne led to a rival claim and eventually to the Wars of the Roses.

1415

Battle of Agincourt

Henry IV's son, the young Henry V, decided to unite his nobles by attacking the common enemy, France. Taking advantage of an escalating civil war across the Channel, Henry led an invading force which met the French army at Agincourt on St Crispin's Day (October 25). The English army of about 6,000 was faced by a French army three times the size, but tactical skill and (once again) the longbow won Henry a glorious victory. He drew up his forces in a muddy field between two woods so that the French assault would be funnelled into a narrow front. The French attacked in three waves. The first wave was beaten off by the longbowmen (70,000 arrows were fired in the first *minute* of the battle); the dead and dying men and horses left in the mud slowed down the second wave, making them even easier targets for the archers. The third wave of men were demoralized by what they saw and did not press home their attack. It was a crushing victory with many thousands of

French killed against just a few hundred English, and it signalled the last period of English dominance in the Hundred Years' War.

1429

Joan of Arc and the Siege of Orleans

Joan of Arc, a nineteen-year-old French girl, saw visions of saints urging her to fight the English invaders. She talked about her visions to the Dauphin (the French king's son), Charles, who believed her (though only after subjecting her to a virginity test) and allowed her to join his armies. She led the French forces to defeat the English and relieve the siege of Orleans, where she was wounded by an arrow. Her daring approach ('Enter, for the city is yours' she cried to her men) as well as her religious enthusiasm inspired the French and their army against the invader. But she was betrayed to the English, who tried her as a witch (one of the accusations was that she wore men's clothes) and burned her at the stake in Rouen. Nevertheless, her martyrdom was the beginning of French revival and led to their eventual victory in the Hundred Years' War, a conflict which marked the final separation of England and France.

Edward III, who started it, was in many ways a French king, but Henry V and Henry VI were born and bred in England and spoke English as their mother tongue.

1450 Jack Cade, an ex-soldier, led 40,000 men from Kent to London to protest about misgovernment, corruption and oppressive taxation. At first the rebels overcame royal forces but then their riotous behaviour upset the Londoners and they were dispersed. Cade was arrested and executed.

1455–85

The Wars of the Roses

The Wars of the Roses, a series of conflicts between two branches of the royal family – the Lancastrians (red rose) and the Yorkists (white rose) – lasted thirty years. The chief cause was the rule of the ineffectual Lancastrian Henry VI, who inherited the throne as a baby (which allowed the nobles on his council to get used to having power) and suffered all his life from periods of extreme depression amounting to madness. It was also unfortunate that in his first decade as an adult king, England finally lost the Hundred Years' War. The country descended into anarchy as powerful barons built up private armies to pursue local feuds. Thinking that Henry was unfit to rule, the Yorkists challenged him and civil war began. The course of the war is confusing. There were some large battles – at Towton in 1461 about 50,000 men were involved – but also many small skirmishes, periods of peace and much political wheeling and dealing, especially by the arch-fixer the Earl of Warwick (the 'kingmaker'). Henry was deposed in

1461, restored briefly to the throne, deposed again and then murdered. The Yorkist Edward IV took over permanently in 1471 and ruled until 1483.

1476

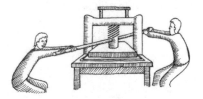

William Caxton and the first Printing Press in England

Caxton was the first man to print books in England at his press in Westminster. The first book printed in England was the *Dictes and Sayings of the Philosophers*, translated from the French. This was followed in Caxton's lifetime by another hundred titles, including Chaucer's *Canterbury Tales* and Malory's *Morte d'Arthur*, as well as many works edited and translated by Caxton himself from Latin, French and Dutch. Caxton had learnt the art of printing in Germany where he had been on business and actually printed several books in English, including *The Game and Playe of the Chesse*, before he returned to London. His early books, which often contained illustrations, were printed in 'Gothic' type on flat bed wooden hand presses, the design of which changed little for the next three centuries. Printing revolutionized intellectual life: books and the ideas they contained were now able to circulate far more quickly.

1483

The Princes in the Tower

When Edward IV died, worn out it is said at the age of forty by his debauched life style, the throne passed to his twelve-year-old son, Edward V. As the boy was too young to rule, his uncle Richard was appointed regent. Richard moved rapidly to take control, arresting young Edward and his little brother, getting them declared illegitimate by Act of Parliament and taking the throne himself as Richard III. The little princes were held in the Tower of London, where they went missing, presumed murdered. There is no actual proof of their death, but they were never seen again and two skeletons of the right size were later discovered in the Tower. Obviously Richard had a lot to gain from eliminating the princes, but it is by no means certain that he was guilty. Some historians have questioned why he did not announce that they had died of sickness or just keep them secure under lock and key. Others have pointed to the fact that it suited the propaganda machine of the Tudors (including, of course, Shakespeare) to portray Richard as a villain.

1485

Battle of Bosworth

Richard III was not to enjoy his kingdom long. Henry Tudor, the leading Lancastrian claimant to the throne, returned from exile in Brittany and gathered an army. The two sides met at Bosworth in Leicestershire. Some of Richard's supporters changed sides at a vital moment and whether or not he cried 'a horse, a horse, my kingdom for a horse', he certainly was killed fighting on foot in a brave attempt to tackle Henry's standard bearer. The story goes that Henry then found the crown hanging on a thorn bush and put it on to become Henry VII. Soon after the battle, Henry married Elizabeth of York, thus uniting the two warring houses.

This is one of those dates that mark a watershed – it is traditionally the end of the medieval period and the beginning of 'early modern' history. It also marks the beginning of a new dynasty – the Tudors. Their emblem, the Tudor rose, containing both red and white, symbolized the end of the struggle between York and Lancaster.

1499 Perkin Warbeck was executed. Warbeck claimed to be the younger of the two princes in the Tower. He was supported by Henry VII's enemies abroad, including James IV of Scotland, whose attempt to invade England and depose Henry failed. This was the final threat to the security of the Tudor dynasty, whose kings and queens ruled England for the next century.

1503 Margaret Tudor married James IV, King of Scotland. Margaret was the daughter of Henry VII, and the marriage created an alliance that led ultimately to the union of the crowns of England and Scotland – ironically, in view of the fact that the Tudor family originally stemmed from Wales.

1509

Henry VIII Becomes King

Just eighteen years old when he ascended the throne, Henry was universally admired for his charm, his good looks, his intelligence, his musicianship and his athleticism – a contrast to his dour father, who had established the Tudor dynasty, created a prosperous economy and accumulated a large personal fortune, but whose cautious and prudent approach to government was never going to set the pulses of his people racing.

Young Henry married his brother's widow, Catherine of Aragon, who bore him a daughter (the future Mary I), and embarked on an ambitious and expensive foreign policy in France and Scotland. His intellectual and religious credentials were underlined by a book he wrote against the position of Luther, the founder of the Protestant reformation, which earned him the title 'defender of the faith' from the Pope – a title which kings and queens of England still bear (the F.D. on coins stands for *fidei defensor*).

1513 Battle of Flodden. When Henry VIII invaded France, James IV of Scotland invaded England despite his marriage to Henry's sister Margaret. The English army inflicted the most crushing defeat ever suffered by a Scottish army at English hands. Possibly as many as 10,000 Scots were killed, including twelve earls, many lords and clan chiefs, and James himself. The haunting bagpipe tune 'Flowers of the Forest' commemorates this disaster for Scotland.

1520 The Field of the Cloth of Gold. Henry arrived in France with 6,000 followers to negotiate an alliance with Francis I of France, a young king whose glamorous reputation as an ideal Renaissance prince rivalled Henry's. The negotiations took place against the background of an extraordinary display of conspicuous consumption. Both sides erected temporary cities of tents and pavilions, covering acres of ground and decorated with silk, cloth of gold and jewels. Balls, plays, feasts, firework displays, jousting and wrestling went on for three weeks as the English and French attempted to outdo each other in the lavishness of the entertainments they offered. In the end no alliance was agreed and within a short while England and France were at war again.

1529

The Reformation Parliament and Henry VIII Divorces Catherine of Aragon

After twenty years of marriage to Catherine of Aragon, during which time she had produced one daughter and no other surviving children, Henry claimed that God's judgment was against him for marrying his brother's widow and that the marriage should be annulled. In fact, his eye had been caught by the sexy Anne Boleyn, who looked capable of providing him with a son and heir but refused to sleep with him unless he married her. The Pope would not agree to annul his marriage to Catherine, so Henry took matters into his own hands. He summoned a Parliament which over the next few years removed the English church from the control of the Pope by declaring Henry 'supreme head of the church and clergy of England' and went on to annul his marriage to Catherine and legitimize his marriage to Anne.

Naturally, not everyone was happy with Henry's high-handedness, but he had a short way with anyone who protested: the most famous of them, Thomas More (*A Man for all Seasons*) was executed for defying the king.

Anne Boleyn gave Henry just one daughter (the future Elizabeth I), and in 1536 she was executed for alleged infidelity. In his search for an heir Henry married four more times, but only Jane Seymour gave him another child (later Edward VI) and died in childbirth. 'Divorced, beheaded, died' were the fates of the first three wives, 'divorced, beheaded, survived' went the last three. They were: Catherine of Aragon, Anne Boleyn, Jane Seymour, Anne of Cleves, Catherine Howard and Catherine Parr.

1530 Cardinal Wolsey arrested. Henry VIII's chief minister was arrested but died before he could be put on trial. He had made himself hugely rich and powerful, but angered the king by failing to support his divorce from Catherine of Aragon. Henry took over Wolsey's splendid residence, Hampton Court, and made it into a royal palace.

1536

The Pilgrimage of Grace and the Dissolution of the Monasteries

Henry faced a serious challenge when the north of England rose in the rebellion known as the Pilgrimage of Grace. The rebels, including powerful noble families, were upset by Henry's oppression of the church and his treatment of the monasteries, which he was in the process of dismantling or 'dissolving' by selling off their lands. The rebels carried religious badges and banners and presented themselves as defenders of the church and the poor rather than rebels against the crown. Henry sent an army to face them with messages of clemency which persuaded the nobles to disperse without fighting. The king later went back on his word and several of the leaders were executed. Henry was certainly not going to stop dissolving the monasteries – getting rid of them was a way to show his control over the church, and the monasteries were great landowners. Henry pocketed the considerable proceeds of selling their property, although as he sold most of it cheaply, the gentry and merchants who bought monastic lands did even better out of the deal.

1549 The first Protestant Prayer Book published. Henry VIII died in 1547 and was succeeded by his sickly ten-year-old son Edward VI, who had been brought up a Protestant and was surrounded by Protestant advisors.

1553 Lady Jane Grey executed. Edward VI died in the same year and his half-sister Mary, a devoted Catholic, succeeded. The Protestant Lady Jane Grey was declared queen but she ruled for only nine days before she was deposed and beheaded.

1555 Latimer and Ridley burned at the stake. Mary restored England to Roman Catholicism and some 300 Protestants were burnt at the stake. Bloody Mary's most famous victims were the bishops Latimer and Ridley and the Archbishop of Canterbury Thomas Cranmer. Latimer's words as the flames licked around the stake to which he and Ridley were tied are unforgettable: 'Be of good comfort, Master Ridley . . . we shall this day light such a candle by God's grace in England as shall never be put out'.

1558

Elizabeth I Becomes Queen

Mary died childless and disappointed, haunted by the loss of Calais to the French ('it will be printed on my heart') and probably killed by the cancerous growth which she had once pathetically interpreted as a sign of pregnancy. Her half-sister Elizabeth had just about managed to keep out of trouble during Mary's reign – not easy for Anne Boleyn's daughter, who had been brought up as a Protestant. But the young woman who now ruled England was a formidable character: she spoke four languages, had a temper to match her red hair, and knew how to manage men – both her counsellors and those who wanted to marry her. She was not short of marriage offers but accepted none of them, preferring as she put it to 'live and die a virgin'. She dealt skilfully with religion, making England a Protestant nation without persecuting Catholics unless they plotted against her – she said 'I have no wish to make windows into men's souls'. She trod a tricky path in Europe, staying friendly with France and avoiding war with Spain until her later years. Despite her love of good living and expensive clothes (her wardrobe contained 1,000 gowns) she avoided running up debts. And she understood the importance of public relations to a successful monarch: Elizabeth was never afraid to show herself to her people and they loved her in return.

1560 The church in Scotland became officially Protestant.

1564

William Shakespeare born

The son of a prosperous glove-maker, Shakespeare was born in Stratford upon Avon, where he was educated at the town's grammar school. At eighteen he married Anne Hathaway, who was eight years older. She was already pregnant with their first child and later bore him twins. The young William went to London to make a career as an actor and playwright. His early plays, including *Richard III* and *The Comedy of Errors*, were instant hits and he became a shareholder in the Lord Chamberlain's Men, a theatrical company which built the Globe Theatre. Plays like *Romeo and Juliet* and *A Midsummer Night's Dream* followed and the company frequently performed for Elizabeth I, as they later did for James I, who granted them the title 'The King's Men'. After producing his final plays, dark tragedies like *Macbeth* as well as sunnier romances such as *The Tempest*, Shakespeare returned to Stratford a prosperous and successful writer and died there on 23 April 1616.

1580 Francis Drake returned to England in his ship the *Golden Hind*, having become the first English-man to sail around the world, a feat which took him more than two years. Queen Elizabeth knighted him on board ship.

1585 Sir Walter Ralegh sponsored the first attempt to found an American colony in Virginia (named in honour of Elizabeth the Virgin Queen).

1587

Execution of
Mary Queen of Scots

As Elizabeth I was childless, the heir to the throne of England was her cousin Mary Queen of Scots, a cultured, charismatic and glamorous woman, but unfortunately also a Catholic with a chequered past. She was an especially poor picker of husbands: number one was the weakling French prince Francis, who then succeeded to the throne of France, making Mary briefly Queen of France as well as Scotland, but he died soon after, probably without ever being able to consummate the marriage. Mary returned to Scotland and married her cousin Henry Darnley, a good-looking but vicious and drunken young man who gave her a son (the future James I of England) and whose behaviour so annoyed the Scots lords that they had him assassinated, possibly with Mary's cooperation. She then burned her boats by marrying number three, the Earl of Bothwell, a rough soldier who most people believed had organized the murder of husband number two. This united the nobles, most of whom were Protestant, against their Catholic queen; they forced her to abdicate in favour of her infant son and imprisoned her. Mary escaped from prison and fled to England to throw herself on the mercy of Elizabeth, whose unsisterly response was to place her under arrest and keep her in a series of fairly comfortable but remote prisons for the next eighteen years. In fact, Mary's presence in England was a constant thorn in Elizabeth's side, because she was a focus for disaffected Catholics who wanted to restore the old religion. A series of conspiracies aimed at freeing Mary and removing Elizabeth from the throne, involving Spain, the Pope and the Jesuits as well as English Catholics, culminated in the Babington Plot of 1586. This was penetrated by Elizabeth's agents, and when letters proving Mary's involvement were produced in evidence, she reluctantly gave her signature to a death warrant for her royal cousin. Mary was beheaded at Fotheringhay Castle; the executioner fumbled his first blow with the axe and had to strike again. When he lifted up the dead woman's head her hair came away in his hand – the once glamorous Queen of Scots had been hiding her grey crop under a wig.

1588

The Spanish Armada

'I know I have the body of a weak and feeble woman, but I have the heart and stomach of a king, and of a king of England too.' Elizabeth's speech to her troops at Tilbury facing a possible Spanish invasion showed her brilliance as a speaker and her ability to capture the national mood of defiance. The uneasy relationship with Spain had finally erupted into war in 1585 when Elizabeth sent her favourite, the Earl of Leicester, with an army to help Protestants in their revolt against their Spanish rulers in the Netherlands. English raids on Spanish treasure ships and colonies in the New World had long caused annoyance, and the final insult was Drake's raid on Cadiz in 1587 when he 'singed the king of Spain's beard' and burned many of the ships which Philip II of Spain was collecting for his attack on England. Given these circumstances, the execution of the Catholic Mary Queen of Scots seemed like a slap in the face to the Spanish king.

Philip sent a fleet of 130 ships with 17,000 men on board through the Channel to rendezvous with the

Spanish army in the Netherlands – the plan was to collect these troops and ferry them across to England as an invasion force. The English navy, commanded by Lord Howard and Sir Francis Drake and roughly the same size as the Armada, harassed the Spaniards as they sailed in tight formation up the Channel, sent fireships in among them when they anchored off Calais and defeated them at the battle of Gravelines. The Armada was then scattered by gales; many ships escaped northwards but were wrecked on the coasts of Scotland and Ireland. Fewer than half made it back to Spain. It was a glorious naval victory for England, even if not quite the victory that Drake and his fellow commanders had hoped for – they were disappointed at their failure to capture more ships and thus make a better profit out of the campaign. English seamanship and gunnery had proved superior, but ultimately it was the weather which defeated the Armada. The contribution of the so-called Protestant wind was recognized in the medal struck soon after: it bore the words 'God blew and they were scattered'.

The defeat of the Armada did not end the war; it went on for another fifteen years, during which time two more Armadas were scattered by storms and English captains continued to treat warfare as a business opportunity – Drake later made over £100,000 from the capture of just one ship carrying gold and silver.

1593 The Tyrone Rebellion in Ireland. Catholic Ireland was nominally under English rule, but the Earl of Tyrone, who was in contact with Spain, started a rebellion. It took ten years to put down, at great cost in lives and money. The rebels' lands were confiscated and taken over by English owners.

1598 The Poor Law was passed by Parliament – the first attempt by the government to provide some sort of relief for the destitute. The 1590s were a desperate time for the poor, with high taxation, trade depression, a succession of harvest failures and recurring plague.

1601 The execution of the Earl of Essex. The ageing Elizabeth's toyboy favourite, the Earl of Essex, overstepped the mark and led a rebellion. Elizabeth showed that she had lost none of her determination by having his head chopped off.

1603

James I becomes king

Elizabeth could never bring herself to name her successor, but everyone knew it would be James VI of Scotland, the son of her old adversary Mary Queen of Scots. In many ways the first Stuart king was an ideal candidate: he was a sound Protestant and an experienced king (he was thirty-seven years old and had ruled Scotland effectively for almost twenty years); he was an ally of England and had been accepting an annual pension from Elizabeth for many years; he had made only a token protest when the mother he hardly knew had been executed; and he had two sons of his own to ensure the succession.

And yet James I of England was not entirely popular with his English subjects and has traditionally had a bad press from historians. This is partly because of his rather unprepossessing personal habits – he 'slobbered at the mouth and had favourites' as *1066 And All That* puts it. He drank too much and ate unattractively; he was fond of handsome young men like George Villiers, Duke of

Buckingham; he wore padded waistcoats because he was terrified of assassination; he was amazingly extravagant and ran up huge debts; his proposal to unite England and Scotland was unpopular; and he followed a foreign policy which seemed too pro-Spanish for many. However, he was also a respected author (his *Counterblast to Tobacco* was an early piece of anti-smoking propaganda), a scholar and an intellectual, a king who took a moderate line in religion and, most of all, kept on reasonable terms with Parliament.

1605

Gunpowder Plot

'Remember, remember the fifth of November' describes probably the only date in British history better known by its month and day than by its year. English Catholics had expected tolerance from James and at first they got it; but when he started to enforce the discriminatory laws against them, a group of young hotheads led by Robert Catesby developed a hare-brained scheme to blow up Parliament when the king was present at its opening – annihilating the monarch, his ministers and all the Lords and Commons in a single explosion. They then planned to raise an army, put the young princess Elizabeth on the throne and bring her up as a Catholic queen.

Guy Fawkes, the man most people associate with the plot, was hired as an experienced soldier and explosives expert. Despite the plotters' lack of organization, the plan came very close to success: the barrels of gunpowder were actually in place before intelligence leaked out to the government. Robert Cecil, the king's chief minister, allowed the conspiracy to go ahead so that the guilty men could be caught red-handed, and Fawkes was arrested in the cellars below Parliament. The other conspirators were soon arrested and executed as traitors. Although the plot was the action of a tiny minority of violent extremists, it was still enough to tar all Catholics with the suspicion of treason for centuries to come.

1607 The first permanent colony in America established in Virginia.

1611 The Authorized Version of the Bible published.

1612 In Ulster land confiscated from Catholic rebels was sold to Protestant Scottish and English settlers.

1620 The *Mayflower*, carrying the Pilgrim Fathers (Puritan emigrants), reached Plymouth in New England.

1625 James was succeeded by his son, Charles I.

1628 The Petition of Right. Parliament presented Charles I with a document called 'The Petition of Right', a list of grievances about heavy taxation and the king's dictatorial rule.

1629–40

The 'Eleven Years Tyranny'

Charles was probably not much more than five feet tall and suffered from a bad stammer. Not surprisingly, he was reserved in manner and stood firmly on his dignity as king. Indeed, he believed implicitly in his divine right to rule – in other words, that he had been chosen by God and that his decisions could not be questioned. Unfortunately for him he needed to call Parliament to grant him money – especially for war – and this gave members of Parliament the chance to criticize his policies. The early part of his reign saw unsuccessful wars, which meant that Parliament met frequently and MPs attacked Charles's chief minister (one of his father's old boyfriends, Buckingham), complained about the way money was raised by 'forced loans' and showed their dislike of the king's religious views. Charles's response was to dissolve Parliament and rule without it.

During the eleven years of his 'personal rule', grievances built up without the safety valve of Parliament to air them. The first of these was religious: Charles favoured a high-church Anglicanism, which looked alarmingly like Catholic worship to many of his subjects, and – what was worse – he put in charge the interfering William Laud, a man who was not averse to resorting to physical mutilation for those who opposed the official line. The second grievance was financial: in the absence of Parliament Charles used a variety of dubious methods to raise money, the most notorious being Ship Money, a tax which coastal counties had always had to pay but which was now extended to inland areas as well. And the third and most important fear was that Charles was going to rule as an absolute monarch and never call Parliament again.

1634 William Prynne was sentenced to have his ears cut off for writing a Puritan pamphlet criticizing theatrical performances at court.

1638 John Hampden, a Buckinghamshire gentle-man who refused to pay Ship Money, was ordered to do so by the judges – but the verdict was only by a majority of seven judges to five.

1639 The First Bishops' War broke out (so called because the Scottish Presbyterians disliked a church run by bishops): Charles and Laud attempted to impose a new high-church prayer book on Scotland (Charles, like his father, was king of Scotland as well as England, but scarcely ever went there). The Scots drew up the

National Covenant to resist the prayer book and raised an army. Charles scraped up the money to send a poorly equipped army north but a few skirmishes achieved nothing.

1640 The Short Parliament. Charles realized that his only hope of raising a good enough army to defeat the rebellious Scots was to recall Parliament and ask it for money. The result was the Short Parliament – it lasted just a few weeks. MPs refused to consider the king's request for help until he dealt with their grievances. When Charles discovered that some MPs, including John Pym, had been in contact with the Scots rebels, he dissolved Parliament and arrested several members. Next, there were riots in London, and rumours about the king's negotiations with Spain and his plans to bring over an army of Irish Catholics. He finally managed to put together an army to tackle the Scots, but before it reached the border it met the Scottish army at Newburn and was utterly defeated. The Scots then occupied Newcastle, putting them in a position to cut off London's coal supply, and demanded a payment of £850 per day until a settlement could be reached.

1640–53

The Long Parliament

Known as 'Long' because it lasted in one form or another for the next thirteen years, this was the Parliament which dismantled the regime of Charles's personal rule, attempted to limit the king's power, fought a war against him, ordered his execution and then ran the country in his place. Its first task was to see to the grievances of the past decade: Ship Money was abolished, Charles's high-church policy was reversed and Charles's hated ministers were imprisoned or executed.

Attempts were made to restrict the powers of the king, but owing to a mixture of the king's stubbornness and Parliament's suspicion of him – a fatal combination – the nation lurched towards civil war. Charles was suspected of planning to restore his powers by a military coup, and Parliament took a range of measures against him, culminating in the Grand Remonstrance, a long list of his illegal acts which was made even more insulting by being published so that ordinary people could read it.

The nation began to split between supporters of the Parliament and the king. The most extreme members of each side were the Roundheads – short-haired, Puritan supporters of Parliament – and the Cavaliers – swaggering, fancily dressed Royalists.

Two events made war almost inevitable: in 1641 a serious rebellion broke out in Ireland. An army had to be raised to deal with it, but neither Parliament nor the king was willing to allow the other to control the army. Then in early 1642 Charles finally attempted the military coup he had long been suspected of planning. He came to Westminster with troops at his back to arrest the five MPs who were his chief opponents, but they had been tipped off ('I see' said Charles, 'the birds have flown') and the coup was a failure. Soon afterwards the king left London, which was becoming too danger-ous for him and his family. He was not to return for another seven years and then it would be to face trial for his life.

1642-46

The First Civil War

The start of the Civil War is traditionally taken to be the moment that Charles raised the royal standard at Nottingham in August 1642, although both sides had been collecting troops and weapons for months. The war faced Englishmen with an agonizing choice and many tried to avoid taking sides at all; there was bewilderment that this 'war without an enemy' was happening at all. But the longer it went on the harder it was fought – the first Civil War and the fighting that followed in the late 1640s and early 1650s caused proportionately more deaths than any other war involving Britain apart from possibly the First World War. In the long run, the odds favoured Parliament: it controlled the richer areas in the south and east; it raised money and ran its war effort more efficiently; it recruited the Scots as allies and created a unified command. Much of the fighting took the form of small skirmishes and sieges of fortified towns or other strong points, but there were a number of set-piece battles.

1642 Battle of Edgehill. In the first major battle of the Civil War two mostly inexperienced armies of about 15,000 men faced each other at Edgehill in Warwickshire. Many on both sides hoped that this would be the decisive and only battle, but in fact it ended in a bloody stalemate. A pattern of events emerged which would become familiar: the Royalist cavalry, led by the king's nephew the dashing Prince Rupert, cut a swathe through its opposite numbers but then rode off in pursuit of the fleeing enemy and started to plunder its baggage train. By the time Rupert returned, the parliamentary infantry was starting to gain the upper hand, but night was falling and the two sides disengaged. If Charles had been more decisive, he could have marched on London, which he had a fair chance of taking, but he failed to act and the opportunity was lost.

1644 Battle of Marston Moor. With nearly 50,000 men on the field near York, this was the battle which gave control of the north of England to Parliament and confirmed the genius of Oliver Cromwell as a commander. In contrast to the indiscipline of the Royalist cavalry, Cromwell's 'Ironsides' broke the enemy's ranks but then wheeled to attack again instead of dashing off in pursuit of plunder. This disciplined approach, together with the assistance of a strong Scots contingent on the parliamentary side, broke the

Royalist army, who lost 4,000 men and all its artillery. Cromwell, with his typical mix of religious zeal and battle-inspired adrenalin said, 'God made them as stubble to our swords'.

1644 Creation of the New Model Army. When the parliamentary generals failed to follow up the victory after Marston Moor, hardliners on the parliamentary side created the New Model Army, which was a properly trained, paid, disciplined and supplied force. Oliver Cromwell was appointed its second in command.

1645 Battle of Naseby. This battle in Northamptonshire proved the effectiveness of the disciplined New Model Army and killed off the king's hopes of winning the war. Prince Rupert, proving himself a liability again, rashly left a strong defensive position to charge the larger parliamentary army. The parliamentarians captured all the Royalist baggage, including Charles's personal papers, among which were letters showing his plans to recruit foreign mercenaries and Irish Catholic soldiers. This discovery, when used in evidence against him, was to play a big part in sealing the king's fate.

1646–8

The Second Civil War

'If we beat the king ninety-nine times, yet he is king still . . .' The Earl of Manchester's words encapsulated the problem which now faced the king's opponents. After Naseby Charles surrendered to the Scots, who quickly sold their royal captive to Parliament. Later the Army – playing an ever greater role in politics – took the king into custody. Charles escaped and threw himself on the mercy of the moderate Parliamentarians. But all the time he was scheming to set his opponents against each other, refusing to accept any deals put to him and plotting to restore his full royal powers. His plans culminated in an agreement with the Scots that they would invade England and join forces with English Royalists, but this so-called Second Civil War was a fiasco. Cromwell marched rapidly north and smashed the Scots at the battle of Preston, and the royalist risings in England were easily put down. Charles was now the

man who had plunged the country back into war –
'Charles Stuart, that man of blood', as his opponents
called him.

1647

The Putney Debates

'The poorest he that is in England has a life to live, as the greatest he . . . it's clear that every man that is to live under a government ought first by his own consent to put himself under that government . . .' These revolutionary (by seventeenth-century standards) words were uttered by Thomas Rainsborough of the Levellers – a radical political movement which was supported by many New Model Army soldiers – in their debate with Cromwell and other army leaders at St Mary's Church in Putney. The Civil War and the attack on established authority which it involved released a flood of new political and religious ideas in England, many well ahead of their time. Contemporaries spoke of the 'world turned upside down' – the established social, political and religious order all threatened with destruction. Some radical movements were relatively mainstream: the Levellers (so-called because they wished to level out social distinctions) were making political demands of a kind which would resurface almost 150 years later at the time of the French revolution; the Quakers (whose unbroken history dates back to this period) believed in pacifism and religious freedom; and even the Diggers' ideas of property held in common were a sort of early communism. Others' ideas were stranger: the Ranters believed that 'to the pure all things were pure' – a doctrine which justified criminal behaviour and sexual licence for those who considered themselves to be God's elect – and the Fifth Monarchists believed that the Civil War was the immediate prelude to the return of Christ to rule on earth. But Cromwell, a country gentleman like most of his fellow parliamentary leaders, had no time for subversive ideas of this kind; he may have fought against the king and favoured religious toleration, but he had no desire to overturn a settled society based on property rights and social distinctions. When the Levellers in the army mutinied they were ruthlessly put down; the Diggers were violently evicted from their commune on St George's Hill in Surrey; and the wilder religious sects were persecuted relentlessly.

1649

The Execution of Charles I

When the Civil War started, the king's parliamentary opponents had no intention of deposing, let alone executing, him – all they wanted to do was to limit his powers and reverse his changes to the church. But his refusal to compromise left them with little choice. Cromwell and other radical parliamentary and army leaders now decided that Charles would have to be got rid of and that this would have to be done in a way that made it look legal. The problem was that many MPs would not agree to take the awful step of putting their anointed king on trial. The solution was to purge Parliament of its moderate members. This task was given to Colonel Thomas Pride, formerly a London brewer and typical of the men of humble birth who had risen through the ranks of the New Model Army. Pride's regiment turned more than 100 MPs away from Parliament, others stayed away on their own initiative and the so-called Rump of members voted to try the king.

In the trial Charles was accused of making war on his own people and destroying 'the fundamental laws and liberties of the kingdom'. In fact, he was being tried by a kangaroo court, set up by a minority of military hardliners, which did not reflect the views of even most of his opponents, let alone of the country at large. He behaved with great dignity – his lifelong stammer left him when he spoke in court – but he made one vital error: instead of pleading not guilty and constructing a defence, which would have spun out proceedings and allowed time for his supporters to rally, he refused to plead or to recognize the authority of the court. This meant that the trial lasted only one week before the court found him guilty and sentenced him to death. The sentence was carried out just three days later. After the axe fell, on a cold January day at Whitehall, the executioner held up the severed head and declared, 'Here is the head of a traitor'; but eyewitnesses reported that from the assembled crowd there came a great groan. Shortly afterwards the Rump Parliament passed Acts abolishing the monarchy and House of Lords and declaring England to be a 'Commonwealth and Free State'.

1649 Cromwell led an army to subdue Ireland. His taking of the towns of Drogheda and Wexford, with subsequent killing of civilians and later massive confiscation of rebels' lands, made him a hate figure in Irish history.

1650 Cromwell defeated the Scots at the battle of Dunbar. His army was outnumbered, but a combination of tactical errors by the Scots and decisive brilliance by Cromwell gained the victory which eventually led to English control of Scotland for the next decade.

1651 The Battle of Worcester. Charles I's son, who had been crowned Charles II in Scotland, led an army into England but this last royalist resistance was snuffed out at the battle of Worcester (called his 'crowning mercy' by Cromwell). The young king escaped from the battlefield and reached exile in France, after adventures on the way which included hiding from Cromwell's soldiers in an oak tree at Boscobel in Shropshire (the 'royal oak').

1653

Cromwell Expels Parliament

'In the name of God, go'. With these words Cromwell used his power as commander-in-chief of the army to dismiss the Rump Parliament and subsequently install himself as Protector. It is tempting to see Cromwell as a military dictator or a king in all but name. Certainly he attempted to impose a moral code on the country, for example by closing the theatres and banning traditional festivals and sports; he also maintained a large standing army and kept taxation high to pay for it. But in other ways he was no dictator: he kept trying to work with some sort of Parliament, he remained committed to religious toleration (for example, he allowed Jews to settle in England for the first time in 350 years) and he could be engagingly informal, as when he asked Lely to paint him 'warts and all'. MPs from all three countries sat in his parliaments and he laid the foundations for British naval supremacy and the future British empire.

1660

The Restoration of Charles II

What Cromwell could not do was to make his regime outlast his own life. When he died in 1658, his ineffectual son Richard ('Tumbledown Dick') took over as Lord Protector but was unable to control the competing ambitions of the army leaders, dedicated republicans and more moderate parliamentarians. Anarchy ensued, and the moderates invited General Monk, the military governor of Scotland, to bring his army down to London and restore order. Monk took things even further by restoring the pre-Cromwellian Parliament, which invited Charles II to return as king.

The rejoicing which met Charles when he returned to England showed that the country had had enough of political experimentation and Puritan dogma, and wanted to get back to old familiar ways. But this did not mean a return to the sort of absolute rule which Charles I had seemed to be constructing. His son was shrewd enough to see this – after all, he had, as he said, no wish to 'go on his travels again' – and the deal he offered was a very moderate one: free parliaments, religious toleration, back pay for the army, pardons for all except a few. In a grisly ceremony Cromwell's body was dug up and hanged, and ten death sentences were passed on men who had signed Charles I's death warrant, but Richard Cromwell was quietly allowed to go abroad. The new king was above all things a survivor, flexible and pragmatic in his approach to ruling, and devoted to pleasure as much as business. He had a famously active sex life, and although his many mistresses, including Nell Gwynn, rarely interfered in politics, they did contribute to his extravagant spending. He had his problems with Parliament over money, religion and his friendship with the absolutist monarch Louis XIV of France, but relations never reached breaking point. Restoration England took its tone from its 'merry monarch'; in strong contrast to the Commonwealth period, it was worldly rather than religious, interested in science (the Royal Society was founded in 1662) and devoted to pleasure. The theatres re-opened and the plays of the Restoration dramatists were flippant, bawdy and cynical, and featured women on stage for the first time.

1665

The Great Plague

'Ring-a-ring of roses . . .' The familiar nursery rhyme dates from this time and refers to the disfiguring marks of bubonic plague. A very hot summer encouraged the plague bacillus (there had been periodic outbreaks for years) to multiply, and medical ignorance only made matters worse – Londoners were encouraged to kill cats and dogs, which were believed to spread plague. The rich, including the king, his court and many doctors and surgeons, fled first. It was tougher for the poor, especially when the authorities started to close the roads to all those who did not have a certificate of health. To contain the disease, the houses of known victims were sealed and guarded and a red cross was painted on the door. Deaths rose to a peak in late summer and the cry 'bring out your dead' became familiar as carts took the bodies off to mass graves. Perhaps as many as 100,000 died in the London area out of a total population of half a million. Winter saw the death rate drop, but it was not until February 1666 that the king considered it safe to return to his capital.

1666

The Fire of London

This was the second catastrophe to hit London in two years, although astonishingly only a handful of people actually died in the fire. It started in a baker's shop in Pudding Lane – the site is still commemorated by the Monument – and spread rapidly through the wooden buildings of the city. At first it caused little alarm – the Lord Mayor said 'a woman could piss it out' – but it soon became obvious that this was fire on a gigantic scale. Samuel Pepys's diaries recorded, 'an entire arch of fire above a mile long . . . it made me weep to see it'.

The king himself took charge of the fire-fighting operation and ordered that buildings be pulled down to make fire-breaks. The fire burned for four days, but was eventually defeated by the tactics of the fire-fighters and a fortunate change of wind which drove it back towards the river. The fire burned the heart out of the old city. More than 13,000 houses and 80 churches were destroyed as were many public buildings, and the heat was so great that the lead from the roof of old St Pauls ran like a stream in the street. In all, over 400 acres of

London were burned. In fact, the fire was a blessing in disguise: Sir Christopher Wren was commissioned to build the new St Paul's as well as over 50 other fine new churches, and the ancient slums which had bred the plague were sterilized by fire and rebuilt in brick and stone.

1667 Milton published *Paradise Lost*.

1675 Sir Christopher Wren's designs for St Paul's Cathedral approved by Charles II.

1677 Charles II's niece Mary married to William of Orange.

1678

Titus Oates and the Popish Plot

A prominent London magistrate, Sir Edmund Berry Godley, was approached by Titus Oates with evidence of a Catholic plot to murder the king, massacre Protestants and bring an army into England from overseas. Oates was not, on the face of it, a reliable informant: he was a disgraced clergyman who has lost several positions after accusations of drunkenness, theft and homosexuality, but his unlikely story suddenly acquired plausibility when Godley was found murdered. A hysterical reaction followed: anti-Catholic pamphlets were published, rumours ran wild and effigies of the Pope were burned in public. Parliament believed Oates's allegations, judges accepted flimsy evidence against Catholic 'conspirators' and a number were executed. A proper investigation later proved that Oates had fabricated the entire thing, but the episode showed the degree of English prejudice against Catholics and contributed to the increasingly popular view that the king's Catholic brother James should not be allowed to succeed him on the throne.

1679 The Habeas Corpus Act was passed. Still in force today, the Act prevents imprisonment without due cause.

1679–81 The Exclusion Crisis. Parliament attempted to pass the Exclusion Act, which was aimed at preventing James from succeeding to the throne. Charles refused to allow this and dissolved Parliament. This was the time the labels 'Whig' and 'Tory' began to be attached to politicians: Whigs wanted to preserve the liberties of Parliament and exclude James, Tories supported the king.

1683 A frost fair was held on the frozen Thames. This was the coldest year of Britain's 'little ice age'.

1685

The Battle of Sedgemoor

Charles II died and the throne went to his Catholic brother, who became James II. This was precisely the outcome which many had feared, and not everyone was prepared to take it lying down. Charles's illegitimate – but Protestant – son, the duke of Monmouth, rapidly assembled an army of volunteers, but few men of rank joined him. When he met the royal army near Bridgwater on Sedgemoor, his ill-equipped troops (known as the 'pitchfork army') were no match for their disciplined opponents. After a crushing defeat, Monmouth was taken to London, tried and executed. Vengeance on those who had supported him was equally savage; rebels came up before the infamous Judge Jeffries, whose sentences were so harsh that these trials became known as 'the Bloody Assizes'. It appeared that James II had now secured his throne, but he soon succeeded in upsetting the majority of his subjects by suspending the laws discriminating against Catholics and appointing many Catholics to high offices. This was to be his undoing.

1687

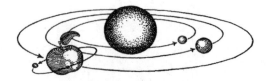

Isaac Newton's *Principia Mathematica* published

Supposedly inspired to develop the theory of gravitation by watching an apple fall to the ground, Isaac Newton wrote this groundbreaking book which is generally seen as the founding text of modern physics. The book introduced scientific concepts such as mass, mechanics (Newton invented the word), calculus and Newton's three laws of motion. For the first time a mathematically proved theory was able to explain the motion of the planets, comets and the moon as well as the tides and the equinoxes.

Newton also published on light (*Opticks*) and in later life devoted himself to the less 'scientific' study of alchemy. His career included spells as an MP, Master of the Royal Mint and President of the Royal Society. Despite his fame and wealth, Newton never married and lived modestly. His epitaph by Alexander Pope says it all: 'Nature, and nature's laws lay hid in night: God said "Let Newton be" and all was light.'

1688

The Glorious Revolution

The removal of James II and the substitution of his daughter Mary and her husband William of Orange was 'glorious', i.e. bloodless, only from an English point of view: considerable blood was later shed in Ireland and Scotland. And it was not really a revolution, merely the exchange of one ruler for another to the benefit of the governing and propertied classes of England. James II was a singularly stupid, insensitive and stubborn man, but that would have been immaterial if he had not been so devoted to the idea of reconverting his kingdom to Catholicism, something which his leading subjects associated with the kind of authoritarian monarchy being practised across the Channel in France. James's attempts to disguise his Catholicism as a policy of religious toleration fooled nobody, and the final straw came when he attempted to prosecute seven bishops who defied him. A group of leading noblemen invited the king's safely Protestant son-in-law William of Orange and his wife Mary to come to England and take the throne. Mary was persuaded to agree after being told that her newly born half-brother was only a commoner's child who had been smuggled into the queen's bedchamber in a warming pan. William duly landed with 15,000 troops at Torbay, and James showed his true colours by losing his nerve, failing even to muster his army and then fleeing to France, pausing only to throw the Great Seal of the realm into the Thames in a ludicrous attempt to sabotage the process of government. The crown was then declared to be 'vacant' and William and Mary were offered the throne as joint sovereigns.

1689

The Bill of Rights

The Bill of Rights was the closest that Britain has ever come to a written constitution. With James II removed and William and Mary on the throne, the so-called Convention Parliament agreed that royal power should be limited in various ways: for example, the monarch was not allowed to suspend the law. Other powers, such as the raising of taxation, were to be exercised only with the agreement of Parliament. The continued existence of parliaments was guaranteed, as was the freedom of speech of MPs. Religious toleration and freedom of worship were allowed, but Catholics and Nonconformists were barred from holding most public offices, including of course the monarchy. The monarch was left with the power to choose ministers and control foreign policy, but Parliament's approval was needed to maintain a standing army. Finally, the crown was guaranteed a regular income (the Civil List, as today) but all other costs of government had to be approved by Parliament. The Bill of Rights marked the beginning of Britain's constitutional monarchy – no subsequent monarch has attempted to act as an absolute ruler.

1690 The Battle of the Boyne. This battle is commemorated by Protestant Orangemen in Northern Ireland every 12 July with marches and demonstrations. Ex-king James attempted a comeback by landing in Ireland with a French army and recruiting support from Irish Catholics, but the discipline, greater numbers and superior firepower of King William's army were too much for the Jacobites (supporters of James); although fighting in Ireland continued for another year.

1692 The Massacre of Glencoe. Generations of Scots have been taught 'never trust a Campbell', and this is the reason why: in one of the most notorious episodes of Scottish history, government soldiers from the Campbell clan turned on their hosts, the MacDonalds of Glencoe, and murdered 38 of them including their chief. Others escaped into the hills, only to die of exposure (it was February). This early piece of ethnic cleansing was deliberately ordered by the Earl of Stair, the Scottish Secretary of State, to punish the Mac-Donalds for failing to take an oath of loyalty to king William – the order to the Campbells was to 'cut them off root and branch and put to the sword all under seventy'.

1704

Battle of Blenheim

In accepting the English throne Dutch William had been particularly interested in using England as a counterweight against the French threat to Holland. Before he died William put together an alliance of Austria, Holland, England and many German states to resist the French attempt to unite the crowns of France and Spain.

The supreme commander of the allied army was John Churchill, Duke of Marlborough (an ancestor of Winston Churchill), and his most famous victory over the French was at Blenheim in Bavaria. Marlborough's generalship was matched by his attention to logistical detail and his skill as a diplomat. A grateful nation rewarded him with the magnificent palace at Woodstock, which is called after his victory. He is also remembered through the words of his vivacious and beautiful wife Sarah, who recorded of her husband in her diary, 'his Grace returned from the wars today and pleasured me twice in his top boots'. Blenheim did not end the war, which went on for another nine years, but it stopped the French advance and prevented France from dominating Europe.

1707

Act of Union between England and Scotland

The crowns of England and Scotland had been united since the reign of James I (VI of Scotland), but the countries were otherwise still independent of each other. England feared that Scotland might fall back under the rule of James II's son and renew the 'auld alliance' with France and so pushed for a full union. The idea was opposed by many Scots – Daniel Defoe (author of *Robinson Crusoe*) wrote 'for every Scot in favour there is ninety-nine against' – but opponents of the union could not coordinate their campaign, and a mixture of promises and bribes from England was enough to get the Act through. Robbie Burns's cynical comment on the Scots MPs was that they were 'bought and sold for English gold'. The Act created a new state, the Kingdom of Great Britain, and a new British Parliament at Westminster; customs dues were abolished and taxation, finance and currency were all harmonized. A new Union flag was made from the crosses of

St George and St Andrew (St Patrick's was added later). Scotland was allowed to keep its own Presbyterian church and its own separate legal system, both of which remain.

1713 Treaty of Utrecht brought to an end the War of the Spanish Succession. Britain gained Gibraltar from Spain, and American territories including Newfoundland from France.

1714 Queen Anne died. Although the poor woman had given birth to seventeen children, only one survived infancy and then died at the age of twelve. Under the Act of Succession (1701) the crown passed to Anne's distant Protestant cousin George, Elector of Hanover, who became George I and the first monarch of the Hanoverian dynasty. He never succeeded in learning English and lived in Hanover for most of his reign.

1715 The Old Pretender landed in Scotland. The accession of the unpopular George was the signal for the Stuarts to attempt a comeback. James II's son, known to history as the 'Old Pretender', landed in Scotland with the aim of raising a rebellion. It was a total failure and he left the country with his tail between his legs just six weeks later, never to return.

1720

The South Sea Bubble

Like the dotcom bubble of 2000 or Wall Street in 1929, the South Sea Bubble was a classic case of overheated financial speculation followed by an almighty crash. The government granted a monopoly in trade with Spanish South American ports to the South Sea Trading Company, which offered shares at £100 each. Lured by the fabled gold and silver of South America, people bought shares avidly and the price started to rise, eventually reaching £1,000. The demand for shares was boosted even more by the company's directors, who set themselves up in lavish offices and talked up their profit forecasts. Buying shares soon became all the rage, and companies were set up by unscrupulous entrepreneurs to undertake a variety of unusual business ventures: 'insuring horses' sounded relatively sensible, but 'making sunshine from vegetables' or 'manufacturing a wheel for perpetual motion' should surely have made investors think twice before parting with their cash. It soon emerged that the South Sea Company was not actually doing much trade. Investors started selling and the share price began to drop, eventually slumping to below its opening price. Thousands of investors were ruined; Sir Isaac Newton lost £20,000 and commented ruefully, 'I can calculate the movement of the stars but not the madness of men'. There was an outcry against the company's managers but most of them had escaped abroad. The crash was a severe blow to the British economy, but it survived because the government intervened to prop up the banking system, and the City of London continued to develop into one of the world's financial powerhouses.

1721 Sir Robert Walpole became the first Prime Minister. George I could not understand what was being said in Parliament and was bored by the details of governing, so Walpole had freedom to head a cabinet which ran the country. Walpole served as prime minister until 1742 and in recognition of his services he was presented with No.10 Downing St, which became the residence of all future prime ministers.

1727 George II succeeded his father as king. Although more a German than an Englishman, he absorbed some English language and culture.

1731 Jethro Tull published *Horse-Hoeing Husbandry,* **a major work of the Agricultural Revolution** which detailed his system for sowing seed mechanically. Also at this time Viscount 'Turnip' Townshend introduced turnips into crop rotation.

1733 John Kay developed the flying shuttle, the first major invention of the Industrial Revolution. It sped up the manufacture of textiles by halving the number of hands needed to operate a loom. This caused hostility from weavers who lost their jobs.

1739 The War of Jenkins's Ear. This short and inconclusive naval conflict against Spain would have been forgotten if it had not been for its catchy name. Captain Jenkins helped persuade Parliament to agree to go to war by showing them his carefully preserved ear which he claimed had been cut off by the Spaniards seven years earlier.

1743 Battle of Dettingen. George II was the last British king to lead his troops into battle in person.

1745

Bonnie Prince Charlie
and the '45

Ever since the Glorious Revolution (1688) there had been abortive attempts to restore James II or his descendants to the throne. The Jacobite cause was kept alive by dislike of King William and the first two Georges, who were seen as foreigners by their British subjects, and by support from France and Spain, who enjoyed making trouble for the British crown. All the Jacobites' previous attempts had failed, but in 1745 they came close to success.

Britain was heavily engaged in fighting the War of the Austrian Succession on the Continent; France promised military support; and the Jacobites had a charismatic new figurehead in the person of Prince Charles Edward, the glamorous grandson of James II, also known as 'Bonnie Prince Charlie' or the 'Young Pretender'.

In the event, the promised French help did not materialize, but Charles went ahead anyway and landed romantically on Eriskay in the Hebrides with just seven followers. The Highland clansmen, resentful at English rule since the union in 1707, flocked to join him. Within weeks he had conquered most of Scotland, posed as king at Holyrood Palace in Edinburgh and defeated a government army at the battle of Prestonpans. The next step was to invade England and make good his claim to the throne by deposing King George. And he nearly made it: the Jacobite army reached Derby, only just over a hundred miles from London, when it became apparent that the English were not going to rise up in support as the Highlanders had done. Even so, Charles might have succeeded if he had pressed on, but he allowed himself to be persuaded that retreat was the only option. Despite another victory at Falkirk, the end of the Jacobite dream came at the battle of Culloden in early 1746, when the Duke of Cumberland's experienced redcoats, aided by many anti-Jacobite Scots, defeated Charles's tired and undisciplined Highlanders. The prince himself became a fugitive in the heather, and despite soldiers combing the hills and a price of £30,000 on his head, he was neither discovered nor betrayed. Eventually he was helped to escape to France by Flora Macdonald, who took him on board a boat to the Isle of Skye disguised as her maid.

1750 Landowners began to use private acts of Parliament to create enclosures – in other words to fence off and partition areas which had been common land. This was opposed by the poor, who relied on the commons for cultivation, grazing and other rights such as gathering firewood. Enclosures improved the efficiency and productivity of farming but also resulted in a drift of population to the cities.

1751 The Gin Act was passed to control the sale of gin. 'Drunk for a penny, dead drunk for two, clean straw for nothing'. This was how the seedy gin shops of the eighteenth century advertised their attractions. Gin was the popular drink of the age, and public drunkenness – as vividly shown in Hogarth's etching 'Gin Lane' – was a major concern.

1752 The change from the Julian to the Gregorian calendar. 'Give us back our eleven days' was the cry of the simple souls who believed that eleven days had literally been removed from their lives (and their pay packets, perhaps) by an act of Parliament. In fact, the change from the Julian to the more accurate Gregorian calendar, which involved 'cancelling' the period between 2 and 14 September, was necessary in order to get the calendar back in step with the seasons of the year.

1755 Dr Samuel Johnson published his *Dictionary of the English Language*. This mighty work, which had taken Johnson and his six assistants eight years to compile, was the first modern dictionary in the sense that it gave the literal meanings of words and their usage in practice, as well as investigating their origins and illustrating their definitions with quotations and references. It helped to fix the spelling of English and remained the standard dictionary for the next hundred years. Johnson was not without a sly sense of humour, as shown by his famous definition of 'oats': 'a grain which in England is generally given to horses, but in Scotland supports the people'.

1756 The Seven Years War broke out. This complicated war, which was caused by competition for trade and colonies and involved fighting in Europe, India, North America and at sea, pitted Britain and Prussia against France and Austria. Britain emerged from the war as a genuine world power in possession of a large overseas empire.

1756–7

The Black Hole of Calcutta
and the Battle of Plassey

The East India Company was founded in 1600 and given a royal charter by Elizabeth I. During the next century 'John Company', as it became known, set up trading posts on the Indian coast, and substantial British communities grew up in Bombay, Calcutta and Madras. Their business flourished, helped by privileges granted by the Mughal Emperor of India, although there was competition in the shape of the French, Dutch and Portuguese. After 1700 the rivalry between Britain and France hotted up. The Nawab (ruler) of Bengal, an ally of the French, occupied the British city of Calcutta and imprisoned soldiers of the East India Company in a dungeon (the infamous Black Hole), where a number of them (some say a couple of dozen, others over a hundred) died from heat and lack of air. Robert Clive, the man charged with avenging their deaths, had an army which was just a fraction the size of the enemy's but he took the precaution of making a private deal with Mir Jafar, the Nawab's commander; when battle was joined at Plassey, even the French artillery were unable to prevent Clive's army from gaining a crushing victory with almost no casualties on the British side. The battle gave Britain control of Bengal, drove the French out of northern India and laid the foundations for the East India Company's rule of most of the subcontinent for the next hundred years.

1759 The Duke of Bridgewater started work on the Bridgewater canal to carry coal from his mines to Manchester. Canal transport of coal and other heavy or fragile goods was vital to the development of the Industrial Revolution.

1759 Capture of Quebec. As in India, so in North America, Britain was faced with colonial rivals in the shape of Spain and France. The most important French base was Quebec, and it was here that Prime Minister William Pitt the Elder directed General James Wolfe's army to attack. Quebec was a formidable fortress, protected by water and by 180-foot cliffs, but it proved not to be impregnable. Wolfe discovered a secret steep path to the heights and led his army up it under cover of darkness. The French came out of their fortified position on to the Plains of Abraham to confront Wolfe and in a brief battle the British infantry won the day. Wolfe himself was killed in the moment of victory, as was the French general Montcalm, but although the French held out for a while in Montreal, the capture of

Quebec proved to be the decisive step in the destruction of French power in North America.

1760 George III succeeded to the throne. George III was the grandson of the previous George and the first Hanoverian king to be born and brought up in England. His patriotism, piety and happy marriage did much to endear him to his British subjects, despite his meddling in politics and the bouts of madness which afflicted him later in life. His accession used to be remembered by the rhyme:

'Seventeen sixty yards in a mile
George the Third said with a smile'.

1764

Invention of the
Spinning Jenny

James Hargreaves, an illiterate weaver and carpenter from Lancashire, invented a machine (named after his daughter) that enabled one operator to spin multiple threads by turning a single wheel – the first technological improvement on the spinning wheel. Hargreaves left it too late to patent his invention and therefore did not profit from it. He was also attacked by weavers, who believed correctly that the machine would put them out of work. Around the same time Arkwright patented the first water-powered textile machine and in 1785 the first steam-powered loom was in operation. But the spinning jenny was to be the key that unlocked the door to the manufacturing revolution and marked the start of the enormous textile industry in north-west England and south-west Scotland.

1768 The first *Encyclopedia Britannica* was published in Edinburgh. This was the great age of Edinburgh, when the classically-inspired New Town was being built and the city was the European centre of science, intellectual enquiry and the arts.

1769 James Watt took out a patent to manufacture steam engines. He was not the inventor of the steam engine but he was the engineer who made it useable in industry, especially for pumping. Steam power became the force that drove the machinery of the Industrial Revolution.

1770 Captain Cook sailed into Botany Bay and claimed Australia for Britain. The first convicts were transported to Australia in 1787.

1773 The Boston Tea Party. A group calling themselves the 'Sons of Liberty', dressed as Mohawk Indians and cheered on by a crowd of supporters, boarded three ships in Boston Harbour and dumped 45 tons of tea over the side. This was the so-called Boston Tea Party, a protest by Americans who objected to the tax which the British government had placed on tea without consulting their American subjects ('no taxation without representation' was their cry).

1775

The American War of Independence

The American colonists became increasingly restive under the rule of a British government thousands of miles away which denied them the right to run their own affairs. Protests grew and when the British authorities tried to confiscate weapons from a group of colonists at Concord a confrontation occurred at nearby Lexington. The 'shot heard around the world' was fired and war began – one which would end in humiliating defeat for Britain.

British troops were fighting far from home and operating across vast distances against a dispersed enemy; they were facing an army which rapidly developed from citizen militias into a professional force under General George Washington; and later in the war the Americans were inspired by the ideals of their Declaration of Independence (1776). A substantial number of colonists remained loyal to Britain; Britain's resources were much greater; and the British navy ruled the seas and could supply and support her army. In effect the conflict looked like a stalemate: it was impossible for the British to finally beat the Americans, but it was equally impossible for the Americans to expel the British. What made the difference was the fact that the conflict soon became a worldwide war. France, Spain and Holland seized the opportunity to come in on the Americans' side and pick off Britain's colonies while she was otherwise occupied. Britain now found herself dangerously isolated and facing a serious threat to her empire and her control of the seas. The final straw came at Yorktown in 1781, when General Cornwallis's army was forced to surrender to a joint French and American force. By the Peace of Versailles (1783) Britain recognized the independence of the new United States of America; there was also a general redistribution of colonies, from which Britain came out worse, losing among others Florida to Spain and Tobago to France.

1776 The American Declaration of Independence drafted by Thomas Jefferson. It has in it the famous lines 'We hold these truths to be self-evident, that all men are created equal, that they are endowed by their Creator with certain unalienable Rights, that among these are Life, Liberty and the pursuit of Happiness.'

1779 Iron Bridge was built in Shropshire. The world's first cast-iron structure.

1783 William Pitt the Younger became Britain's youngest Prime Minister, at the age of 24. A Tory, Pitt restored the economy to a sound footing by reducing the national debt and cut out much waste and corruption in government. He also led the country in war against France. Despite his successes and his popularity, Pitt's private life was unhappy: he never married, had no close friends and died at the age of 47, an alcoholic and with enormous debts.

1787 Impeachment of Warren Hastings, the governor-general of India. Hastings was the last man to be impeached (tried by Parliament for crimes committed while in government service). He was eventually acquitted of all charges but ruined by the cost of defending himself.

1788 George III went mad. His doctors' drastic remedies, such as bleeding, blistering and dosing with laudanum, had no effect. Pitt managed to delay the appointment of Prince George as Regent, because he knew that the Prince favoured Pitt's enemy Charles James Fox and the Whigs. Fortunately for Pitt, the king recovered his sanity.

1791–2

Tom Paine's *The Rights of Man* published

The Rights of Man contained an appeal to Britons to rise up and overthrow their monarchy, as the French had done. Paine was charged with treason, but managed to get away into exile in France and the USA. However, many Britons were excited by Paine's ideas, such as votes for all men and a kind of welfare state. In the government's eyes the danger was that these notions were getting through to ordinary working men, who began to form so-called Corresponding Societies to discuss politics and spread information. Political power was seen to be for the aristocratic charmed circle, not for the man in the street; and when protest began to become more extreme as a result of poor harvests, high prices and unemployment, Pitt's government hit back by prosecuting leading radicals, suspending habeas corpus (so allowing arrests without charge) and passing repressive laws such as the Seditious Meetings Act to restrict the activities of the radicals. Radical protest died down, partly because economic conditions improved and partly because France, the source of revolutionary ideas, became the enemy in war, making radical notions look unpatriotic.

The year 1792 also saw the publication of Mary Wollstonecraft's *Vindication of the Rights of Women*, a plea for women's education and equality of the sexes. But she was far ahead of her time and it would be more than another half century before women made any real steps towards equality.

1793 Revolutionary France declared war on Britain. War was inevitable when France invaded Belgium and threatened to occupy the coastline of the Low Countries, a strategically and commercially vital area for Britain.

1796 Discovery of vaccination. Edward Jenner used vaccination (inoculation with material taken from cows' udders) against smallpox for the first time, having noticed that dairy maids had unblemished complexions.

1798 Battle of the Nile. Nelson totally destroyed a French fleet at the mouth of the Nile. His daring tactics – attacking at dusk and sailing between the anchored French ships and the shore – won the one-armed, one-eyed admiral a huge following in the navy and immense fame with the public.

1798

Wolfe Tone's rebellion in Ireland

Three-quarters of the land in Ireland was owned by Protestants, many of them English absentee landlords. The government of Ireland was directed from London and represented in Ireland by the so-called Protestant Ascendancy of magistrates, landowners and officials; although there was an Irish Parliament, Catholics were not allowed to be members. The bulk of the population were Catholic peasants, who had no political rights at all and lived in desperate poverty, as bad as any in Europe at the time and made worse by rapid population growth. Arson and cattle-maiming were common ways for the Irish poor to protest against their exploitation by landlords.

Discontent was stoked by the revolutions in America and France – if the Americans could throw off British rule and the French could get rid of their monarchy, then surely the Irish could do it too. The leader who emerged was Wolfe Tone, a lawyer (and surprisingly a Protestant) who founded the Society of United Irishmen to agitate for political reform. This was dangerous enough in British eyes, but even worse was the fact that Tone was in cahoots with Britain's enemy, the French. Not for the last time, 'England's difficulty was Ireland's opportunity'. But the rebellion itself proved to be a bloody failure for the nationalist cause: the French did not succeed in landing the promised army, spies and informers betrayed the United Irishmen and British military efficiency proved superior to the revolutionary enthusiasm of the Irish. Many rebels were executed – Wolfe Tone cut his own throat with a penknife to escape the gallows – and in 1801 the Act of Union was passed, abolishing the Irish Parliament and creating the new United Kingdom of Britain and Ireland. The Protestant ascendancy remained in control of Ireland, and it would be decades before any rights were granted to Catholics.

1802 The Peace of Amiens created a brief truce in the war with France. William Pitt's tactics in the war had been to build up the British navy in order to tackle France at sea and in her colonies, and to support allies like Austria with huge financial subsidies. The British army had seen little action and had had even less success.

1805

The Battle of Trafalgar

In 1805, the French admiral Villeneuve gave orders to his fleet, the battleships of the French and Spanish navies, to sail out of Cadiz harbour. The decision may have been provoked by injured pride – Napoleon, who by now had made himself Emperor of France, had threatened Villeneuve with the sack and hinted that he was afraid to face the British navy. Anyway, it was a mistake.

Off Cape Trafalgar Nelson was waiting for the enemy, and again his tactical brilliance won the day: having first hoisted the immortal signal 'England expects that every man will do his duty', he ordered his fleet to divide into two columns and attack the French line from the side, thus splitting them into three. The British ships had to face damaging fire from the enemy broadsides as they closed in, but as soon as they got to close quarters superior British gunnery achieved an overwhelming victory, taking or sinking most of the French and Spanish ships. At the height of the battle, Nelson was hit by a musket ball and carried below. He survived just long enough to hear from his loyal flag captain Hardy that the victory had been won. Trafalgar was the most important naval battle in British history: the French navy was destroyed, Napoleon's plans to invade Britain were gone for ever and Britain's command of the sea was assured for the next hundred years. Nelson himself was mourned as a national hero. Stories about the man and the 'Nelson touch' were already common: how at the battle of Copenhagen (1801) he ignored the signal to withdraw, putting the telescope to his blind eye and saying 'I see no signal'; his notorious affair with the voluptuous Emma Hamilton; and the way he was idolized by his officers and adored by the common sailors. In fact, he was a curious mixture of qualities: vain of his reputation and childishly eager for honours, ruthless in battle, shamefully neglectful of his deserted wife, but also kind and gentle in personal relations and humane as a commander.

1807 Abolition of the Slave Trade. The slave trade was abolished in all British territories (but slavery itself still existed in the British West Indies). The British navy attempted to act as a police force to suppress other countries' trade in slaves.

1809 Arthur Wellesley was created Viscount Wellington, in recognition of his victory over the French at the battle of Talavera in Spain. The Peninsular War (1809–13) was the main theatre for the British army: in alliance with Portuguese and Spanish regular troops and guerrillas, Wellington gradually got the better of the French armies, creating a 'running sore' for Napoleon in the Iberian Peninsula, and by the end of 1813 he had crossed into south-west France.

1811 King George III went terminally mad. His son George was formally appointed Prince Regent and this marked the beginning of the 'Regency' period in art, design and fashion.

1812 Luddite Riots. Unemployed textile workers invaded factories in the North and smashed the new machinery which had taken over their jobs. They were known as Luddites after their mythical leader, 'General' Ned Ludd.

1813 Jane Austen's *Pride and Prejudice* was published – although the book's author was anonymous ('by a lady') and it was only after Austen's death in 1817 that her name appeared on the novels.

1815

The Battle of Waterloo

'A damned nice thing – the nearest run thing you ever saw in your life,' Wellington said about his great victory. If the result had gone the other way European history would have been radically different.

In 1814 Napoleon had been forced to abdicate and was banished to the island of Elba; but he escaped, instantly rallied the veterans of the French army to his cause and reached Paris in just nineteen days. The only serious obstacles facing him were the mixed force of British, Belgians, Dutch and Germans commanded by Wellington and the Prussian army commanded by Blucher; and he believed that if he could keep the two apart, he could defeat them both. In fact, he thought he *had* defeated the Prussians, but he failed to follow up the victory, so that Wellington was able to go into battle at Waterloo, near Brussels, with the assurance from Blucher that the Prussian army would join him. As it turned out, the Prussians did not arrive until mid-afternoon, by which time the battle was already largely won. As usual with Wellington, this was down to a combination of superb planning, for example his choice of fortified strongpoints, and sheer bloodyminded determination. 'Hard pounding this, gentlemen,' he said to his staff during a fierce artillery duel, 'let us see who will pound the longest'. He had succeeded in occupying the higher ground on the battlefield, meaning that the French, who took most of the offensive in the early stages, had to attack uphill through a rather boggy valley. But the British infantry repulsed all the French attacks, including the final assault of Napoleon's Imperial Guard; and when Blucher's Prussians appeared, defeat became a rout.

Waterloo put paid to Napoleon for good: he was dispatched to the safely remote island of St Helena. It also put an end to more than twenty years of war. The peace settlement which emerged at Vienna concentrated on restraining France and establishing a stable balance of power in Europe. Britain gained colonies of strategic importance such as Malta, St Lucia and the Cape Province of South Africa; France was no longer able to challenge British power in India or elsewhere because the British navy ruled the seas. The British economy had survived the war and Napoleon's attempts to strangle it by blockade and the scene was set for Britain to become the world superpower.

1819

The Peterloo Massacre

Twenty-two years of war had masked but not removed the social, economic and political grievances which radicals had aired in the last decade of the eighteenth century. With peace came economic depression as the army and navy paid men off and industry lost the stimulus of wartime government contracts. Unemployment rose and wages fell. Lord Liverpool's Tory government showed no interest in political reform and did virtually nothing to help the poor and destitute; in fact, it seemed to actively make things worse by passing the Corn Law, which protected the interests of its landowning supporters by banning the import of cheap foreign grain – thus raising food prices. Protest took a variety of forms: mass meetings, marches, agitation by political clubs, and even at one point a harebrained plot to assassinate the entire cabinet. The government's response was to crack down hard: leading radicals were arrested, spies were used to infiltrate political clubs, laws were passed to restrict public meetings, and habeas corpus was suspended. The climax came at St Peter's Fields in Manchester. A crowd of at least 50,000 assembled to listen to speeches by radical orators on themes such as 'Votes for all men' and 'No Corn Laws'. The local authorities panicked and sent in the yeomanry (mounted volunteers) to disperse the meeting. The upshot was an ugly brawl which left eleven people dead and hundreds injured. This was the battle sarcastically named 'Peterloo', in reference to the great victory of four years earlier. Liberal opinion was outraged. The poet Shelley attacked the government as, 'Rulers who neither see nor feel nor know/ But leechlike to their fainting country cling.' However, the revolution which many feared did not come to Britain, partly because the army remained consistently loyal and obedient to the government and partly because the radicals were unable to present a united front.

1820 Mad king George III died and the Prince Regent became king as George IV. An exceptionally self-indulgent, greedy and vain individual (he loved dressing up, despite becoming very fat in later life) and capable of immense self-delusion (he regularly claimed falsely to have fought at Waterloo), he was also a man of some wit and culture and a considerable patron of the arts.

1821 Constable painted *The Haywain*, the iconic image of peaceful, rural England – which was far from the way it really was.

1823 Rugby football began when William Webb Ellis, during a game of football at Rugby School, picked up the ball and ran with it.

1824 The RSPCA was founded. The first such organization to be founded anywhere in the world – a tribute to the British love of animals, but also evidence of the growing influence at this time of Evangelical Christianity on British manners and morals.

1825 The Stockton–Darlington railway started operating, the first in the world.

1829 The Metropolitan Police Force was founded by Home Secretary Sir Robert Peel. Its men were therefore known as 'bobbies' or 'peelers'.

1830 George IV died and was succeeded by his brother William IV. Known as the 'sailor king' because of his service in the navy, he had mildly liberal views but not much in the way of brains or character.

1832

The Great Reform Act

Radical protest died down during the 1820s as the economy improved, but the radicals' central demand – for reform of Parliament – did not go away. As things stood, they had plenty to complain about: fewer than 10 per cent of men had the vote, many large towns were not represented in Parliament, and many parliamentary seats were 'rotten' or 'pocket' boroughs, in other words had a tiny number of electors and were controlled by a big landowner. Old Sarum, for example, had just three houses and eleven voters. In 1829 the government had finally granted Catholics the right to become MPs, thus showing that reform of the system was possible. The economy took a downturn in the late 1820s, leading to an increase in support for protest movements. And then a leadership crisis in the ruling Tory party brought the Tory Duke of Wellington into power as Prime Minister. This was desperate news for reformers because Wellington was known to be totally against any reform of Parliament. A two-year political crisis ensued, during which both Wellington and Earl Grey, the Whig leader, held power at different times. With Wellington in power the country appeared to be heading for revolution as protest riots erupted; but when Grey tried to pass a bill to reform Parliament, he could not get it through the Tory-dominated House of Lords. Eventually Grey persuaded King William to agree to create enough new peers to get a reform majority in the Lords, the Lords gave way under this threat and the Great Reform Act was passed. The act removed the rottenest boroughs and redistributed seats to areas which were under-represented; but even this increased the electorate to only about 20 per cent of men. This was Grey's aim of course: he was by no means a democrat, and what he had achieved was to bring the middle classes within the system, thus cutting the dangerous link between the mass protest movement and its middle-class leaders. As Grey himself admitted, 'the principle of my reform is to prevent the necessity for revolution'. None of this prevented the reactionary Wellington from commenting, as he viewed the first House of Commons elected under the new system, 'Never saw so many shocking bad hats in my life'.

1833 Slavery was abolished in all British territories – chiefly sugar plantations in the West Indies. This was the final triumph for the movement started by William Wilberforce more than forty years earlier. However, the slave-owners were compensated with £20 million of taxpayers' money and freedom was granted to slaves only after a transition period.

1834 The 'Tolpuddle Martyrs', agricultural labourers who formed an illegal trade union, were sentenced to transportation to Australia. This was a reminder that although the 'age of reform' was under way, the ruling classes were still afraid of revolution by the poor.

1835 The Municipal Corporations Act was passed, creating elected local government in towns and cities.

1837 William IV died and because he had no legitimate children (he had plenty who were illegitimate) was succeeded by his eighteen-year-old niece Victoria. This determined and serious-minded young woman was to reign for the next sixty-four years and give her name to an era.

1838 Isambard Kingdom Brunel launched his steamship the *Great Western* on her maiden voyage to New York. Brunel was the greatest engineer of the nineteenth century and was to go on to build two even bigger steamships, as well as the many bridges, tunnels and other works involved in the creation of his masterpiece, the Great Western Railway from London to Bristol.

1840 The penny post was introduced. Rowland Hill's idea of a pre-paid adhesive label (a stamp) was an instant winner, and within ten years almost 350 million letters were being sent every year stamped with 'penny blacks' and 'penny reds' bearing the head of the young Queen Victoria.

1841 A census showed that the population of Britain had reached 27.5 million, an increase of 50% since 1800.

1842 Income tax was first levied in peacetime. The top rate was 10% and only the relatively rich were liable to pay it.

1844 Railway mania at its height. Large numbers of railway companies set themselves up in business and railway shares became the hottest stock to own. Inevitably, some of the companies were run by rogues and some investors lost their money, but the mania resulted in Britain being rapidly covered with an extensive rail network. It was also at this time that the telegraph started to be used – so goods, people and information were now all capable of being transmitted at unprecedented speed.

1845

Irish Potato Famine

The potato crop in Ireland was almost totally destroyed by blight. Ireland's exploding rural population was able to support itself on tiny peasant plots only by living almost exclusively on potatoes. In much of the country there was no employment except on the land, and most peasants used the other crops they grew to pay the rent. The blight returned in 1846 and an already weakened population was now dying of starvation and disease in large numbers. People tried to stay alive by eating grass and nettles, whole families died together, and corpses were burned in mass graves. The British government at first left the relief effort up to the local authorities in Ireland, then set up public-works schemes to provide employment and finally sent in food aid and organized soup kitchens. But the effort was too little too late, and communications in underdeveloped Ireland were so poor that actually getting help to the starving was not easy. By 1850 almost a million men, women and children had died, and in the next two decades another two million emigrated.

1846 Repeal of the Corn Law. It seemed obscene to have an import tax on food (the Corn Law) when thousands of people were starving to death in Ireland. The prime minister of the day, Robert Peel, abolished the Corn Law but at the cost of splitting his own Conservative Party, which was to remain in the political wilderness for most of the next thirty years.

1847 The Ten Hours Act banned women and young people (aged 13 to 18) from working longer than a ten-hour day in textile factories. Other laws protecting factory employees had been passed since the 1830s, but children as young as nine were still going out to work.

1849 Charles Dickens published *David Copperfield*. Dickens was the first truly popular novelist in English and his works were made more accessible by being published in instalments in monthly magazines.

1851

The Great Exhibition

By the mid-nineteenth century Britain was calling herself 'the workshop of the world' and the national mood of self-congratulation was perfectly expressed in the Great Exhibition, held in Hyde Park. The idea, promoted by Queen Victoria's husband Prince Albert, was to hold the biggest ever exhibition of 'the works of industry of all nations' – it was, in other words, a combination of a show for the curious public, a competition for manufacturers (prizes were offered) and a shopping experience. It certainly was big: for the main exhibition hall Joseph Paxton designed an iron-framed glass building covering nineteen acres and containing over a million square feet of glass. And it was a huge success: over six million visitors came during the five months it was open, and the profits helped to fund the building of the Victoria and Albert, Science and Natural History Museums. Although there were exhibits from all over the world, more than half were British.

1854–56

The Crimean War

Between 1815 and 1914 the Crimean War was the only war in which Britain took on another European power. The issue at stake was how to stop Russia conquering the crumbling Turkish empire and so dominating the eastern Mediterranean, the Middle East and the road to British India. Britain and France, allies for the first time in almost three hundred years, sent a joint force through the Black Sea to attack Russian ports in the Crimea. Public opinion was all for war at the start – the Russians were seen as brutal and uncivilized – but it rapidly became apparent that the British army, after forty years of peace, was grossly unprepared. The British commander Lord Raglan had seen no active service since Waterloo and could not break the habit of referring to the enemy as 'the French'. It was Raglan's order, misunderstood by the bone-headed Lord Cardigan, which led to the gallant but hopeless charge of the Light Brigade straight into the mouths of the Russian guns. The battles of Balaclava and Inkerman were hard-won victories, but not decisive enough to polish off Russian resistance. It was the Russian winter which revealed the horrifying incompetence of the British command: there were desperate shortages of food, medical supplies, fuel, shelter and basic equipment such as boots. Disease killed more men than died in battle, and even the heroic efforts of Florence Nightingale and her nurses at the Scutari hospital could not undo all the damage. The war dragged on pointlessly until Russia made peace by agreeing to respect Turkish independence and allowing the Black Sea to be a neutral area – promises which were broken fewer than twenty years later. The Crimea was the first war which the public at home could follow in detail because war correspondents sent their despatches back by telegraph. Their revelations of incompetence led to some improvements in the life of ordinary soldiers, but little was done to tackle the problem of incompetent aristocratic commanders.

1857

The Indian Mutiny

The mutiny began when Indian soldiers (sepoys) at Meerut refused to obey orders, shot their British officers and marched to Delhi with the aim of restoring the last Mughal emperor and expelling the British from India. The mutineers were joined by many other sepoys from the army of Bengal as well as a good many civilians in northern and central India (the mutiny was never a national movement: some parts of India were unaffected and many sepoys remained loyal). For some months the British presence was reduced to isolated and besieged garrisons – Lucknow was the most famous example – until a reinforced British army, with the help of loyal Indian troops, succeeded in putting the mutiny down, restoring order and recapturing Delhi. Both sides committed terrible atrocities: the British were especially shocked by the sepoys' murder of women and children, but their retaliation was equally savage. In revenge for the massacre of 200 British women and children at Cawnpore, nearly 2,000 sepoys were slaughtered, many by being blown from cannons. What set the mutiny off was the issue to the sepoys of new cartridges, which were believed to be greased with pig and cow fat – therefore unclean to both Muslims and Hindus. But the underlying cause was the way the British ruled India: in the eighteenth century the East India Company had taken a 'hands off' line – do business but don't interfere with the customs of the country. However, this was not the Victorian way: as well as increasing taxation, the British were now trying to change age-old Indian traditions by encouraging Christian missionaries, reforming the legal system and introducing Western education. The mutiny was a considerable psychological shock to Britain and caused a great change of heart towards India. Do-gooding sympathy for Indians was transformed into suspicion and hatred; attempts to 'improve' the Indian way of life or impose Christian and Western values became less popular; a barrier went up between British and Indians; and the rule of the East India Company was abolished and replaced by direct rule from London.

1858 The Great Stink. The smell from the polluted Thames became so bad that Parliament was forced to halt proceedings. London still lacked an efficient sewage system and cholera epidemics had been common in recent decades. The problem was solved by Joseph Bazalgette, who built over 1,000 miles of new sewers and main drains.

1859 Charles Darwin published *On the Origin of Species by Means of Natural Selection*. This great work, the textbook of evolution, was violently attacked by many Christians and keenly defended by most scientists. 'A man has no reason to be ashamed of having an ape for his grandfather', declared T H Huxley, in reply to creationist Bishop Wilberforce.

1861 Prince Albert died of typhoid, caused by the primitive sanitation system of Windsor Castle. Queen Victoria entered a long and morbid period of mourning, during which she withdrew from public life. The monarchy consequently became very unpopular, until Victoria was enticed back into the spotlight by Prime Minister Disraeli in the 1870s.

1863 The Football Association founded. Twelve clubs and schools met to draw up an agreed set of rules for the game. Within a decade the first FA Cup competition took place.

1864 The opening of London's Metropolitan Railway led to the growth of suburban housing and the birth of the commuter.

1865 Elizabeth Garrett Anderson became the first woman in England to qualify as an apothecary. Later, she qualified as a doctor in Paris, returning to practise in England; but women could not qualify as doctors in England until the 1870s, most universities did not admit women until after 1880 and women could not qualify as barristers or solicitors until the 1920s.

1867

Disraeli and the Second Reform Act

This act gave the vote to many working-class town-dwellers, bringing the proportion of men who had the vote up to about 40 per cent. The man responsible for getting it through Parliament was Benjamin Disraeli, who shortly afterwards became Conservative prime minister, thus reaching, in his own words, 'the top of the greasy pole'. It might seem strange that the Conservative Party was responsible for such a drastic reform, but then Disraeli was far from being a normal Conservative. Born into a Jewish family at a time when Jews were still unable to become MPs, his early career was as a successful novelist and fashionable man about town. He first stood for Parliament as a Radical, but at his fourth attempt was elected as a Tory. His political skills and his debating ability were soon recognized, but it was difficult for a Conservative Party which was still predominantly made up of the landed gentry and aristocracy to come to terms with having an 'outsider' like Disraeli as their leader.

As prime minister in the 1870s he followed a policy of 'Tory democracy' or 'one nation Toryism' – a mixture of social reforms and an aggressive foreign policy which was claimed to be in the interests of all the people – but became increasingly interested in foreign affairs, expanding the British empire and cultivating the company of Queen Victoria. Two typical gestures were his purchase for Britain of a half-share in the Suez Canal and his creation of the title 'Empress of India' for the queen. He was the queen's favourite prime minister, no doubt because he followed his own advice: 'everyone likes flattery; and when it comes to Royalty you should lay it on with a trowel'. He was a superbly witty writer and speaker, who often exercised his wit at the expense of political opponents, especially Gladstone, the Liberal leader. Disraeli described the Liberal front bench as 'a range of exhausted volcanoes' and Gladstone as 'a sophistical rhetorician, inebriated by the exuberance of his own verbosity'.

1868

Gladstone Becomes Prime Minister

Disraeli's great opponent, William Gladstone, was a very different kettle of fish. When he became prime minister for the first time he spoke of God's purpose for him and declared, 'my mission is to pacify Ireland'. Although he achieved some changes to religion and land-holding in Ireland, he failed in his ultimate aim – Home Rule for the Irish – because he could not sell it to his own party or get it through a hostile House of Lords. Gladstone was an unusual example of a politician who became more radical as he got older: he first entered Parliament as a Tory, but by the time he became prime minister he was known as 'the people's William'; when he was nearly eighty and prime minister for the third time he declared, 'all the world over, I will back the masses against the classes'; and at the age of eighty-four, and prime minister for the fourth time, he made his final attempt to achieve Irish Home Rule. Christian moral principles were what drove Gladstone in his private and public life: he spent many evenings in London 'rescuing' prostitutes from the street – and then whipping himself as a punishment when he felt desire for them. His speeches tended to be more like sermons; the queen, who could not bear him, said, 'Mr Gladstone speaks to me as if I was a public meeting'. Despite failing with Ireland, he did succeed in putting into practice Liberal ideas of fairness and equality of opportunity: he established a national system of education, abolished the purchase of commissions in the army, introduced competitive entry to the higher ranks of the civil service and made voting in parliamentary elections secret. In foreign affairs his moral approach was less successful: his belief in the 'concert of Europe' as the peaceful means of settling disputes was shaken by Russian aggression and the wars caused by the unification of Germany; and he got drawn into colonial wars in Egypt and South Africa, as well as unwillingly presiding over a great expansion of the British empire.

1870 The Married Woman's Property Act gave wives legal control of any earnings or property they acquired after marriage. A further Act in 1882 gave them control of anything they owned or earned at the time they married. Before these Acts a husband had automatic control of his wife's property.

1871 Stanley found Dr Livingstone. 'Dr Livingstone, I presume,' was how the journalist Henry Stanley greeted explorer and missionary David Livingstone when he found him near Lake Tanganyika in East Africa. The greatest newspaper scoop of all time.

1873 Conquest of the Ashanti kingdom. General Garnet Wolseley led a force to the Gold Coast (now Ghana). The Ashanti kingdom was trying to expel British traders from its coastline, but its army could not stand up against European weapons.

1876 Samuel Plimsoll MP sponsored the Merchant Shipping Act which created the 'Plimsoll Line', painted on cargo ships to show the limit to which they could be legally loaded. Amazingly, one-half of the world's merchant steam tonnage was British.

1878 'We don't want to fight, but by jingo if we do, we've got the ships, we've got the men, we've got the money too!' This year's music hall hit, which gave birth to the word 'jingoism', was directed against Russia's threat to British interests in the Middle East.

1879

Rorke's Drift

A British force of 140 men held off the attacks of 3,000 Zulus at an isolated missionary station in South Africa. Eleven Victoria Crosses (the highest number for any one action) were awarded for this gallant defence, which was the subject of the film *Zulu*.

Britain's aim was to create a Confederation of South Africa under British rule, but two obstacles stood in the way. The first was the Boer republics (*see* 1899). The second was the Zulu kingdom, with its well-trained and formidable standing army of 40,000 men. It was not the British government's intention to go to war against the Zulus, but the 'man on the spot', Sir Bartle Frere, the High Commissioner in South Africa, deliberately provoked war by delivering to the Zulus an ultimatum to disband their army, which made war inevitable.

The first battle was a disaster for the British army and its bungling commander Lord Chelmsford: showing a mixture of over-confidence and contempt for his 'savage' enemy, Chelmsford split his forces and left them open to a surprise attack at Isandlwana by the Zulu king Cetshwayo with 20,000 warriors. Using their traditional encircling tactics (the 'horns of the buffalo') the Zulus virtually wiped out the British force. This was a staggering shock to Britain, used as it was to easy victories over native opponents with inferior weapons. The next day, the much smaller British force survived at Rorke's Drift, but British victory arrived only when Chelmsford was replaced by the all-purpose imperial general, Garnet Wolseley, who defeated the Zulus at the battle of Ulundi.

The Zulu war was a particularly violent episode in what came to be called 'the scramble for Africa' – in other words, the extraordinary decades up to 1900 during which all of Africa except Liberia and Ethiopia came under the rule of European powers. Britain, with extensive holdings in all parts of the continent, is often said to have acquired 'the lion's share'.

1882 A British fleet bombarded Alexandria in response to a nationalist rebellion against foreign influence in Egypt. After victory at the battle of Tel el Kebir Britain occupied Egypt and the Sudan and they became colonies in all but name.

1884 The Third Reform Act gave the vote to agricultural labourers. About two-thirds of all adult males were now eligible to vote.

1885 General Gordon killed at Khartoum. Gordon was sent to Sudan after Mohammed Ahmed, who called himself the Mahdi (Messiah) and was backed by his army of 'dervishes', proclaimed a holy war against the Egyptian and British colonizers. Gordon was besieged in Khartoum and killed two days before a relief force (led by Garnet Wolseley, again) reached the city.

1887 Queen Victoria celebrated her Golden Jubilee. Fifty foreign kings and princes attended the celebrations. Many of them were related to the queen, and the gathering also included many Indian rajas.

1888 Fourteen hundred women employed in Bryant and May's match factory went on strike in protest against working hours and conditions, including the danger of contracting bone cancer ('phossy jaw') from the phosphorus used in the manufacture of match heads. Their strike was successful and was an inspiration for unskilled workers to form trade unions.

1892 Keir Hardie, a Scottish miner, was elected to Parliament as the first Labour MP. Hardie, the illegitimate son of a servant girl and completely self-educated, created a sensation by turning up in the House of Commons in a working man's cloth cap and tweed suit – at a time when the conventional dress for MPs was top hat and tail coat.

1896 The *Daily Mail* started publication. Costing just a halfpenny (rival newspapers were all priced at a penny), it soon achieved a circulation of half a million. A strongly patriotic line on news together with plenty of competitions and human interest stories made it a popular and easy read.

1898 Battle of Omdurman. General Kitchener defeated the forces of the Mahdi (*see* 1885) at the battle of Omdurman and reconquered Sudan for Britain. Although British forces were outnumbered two to one, the superior weaponry of the British won the day. Hilaire Belloc commented, 'Whatever happens, we have got/ The Maxim gun, and they have not'. The young Winston Churchill was present at the battle and rode with the 21st Lancers in the last full-scale cavalry charge ever mounted by the British army.

1899–1902

The Boer War

South Africa had originally been colonized by the Dutch, and the descendants of those settlers – known as Boers ('farmers') – had established two independent republics in Transvaal and Orange Free State. They stood in the way of Britain's aim to unite southern Africa under British rule. The discovery of gold and diamonds in the Transvaal simply made a British South Africa a more desirable prospect. The gold rush bought large numbers of foreigners (known to the Boers as 'uitlanders') into the Transvaal; on the pretext that the Boers were denying political rights to the uitlanders, the British delivered increasingly demanding ultimatums which finally drove the Boers into declaring war.

The early battles were a shock for the British army: it suffered a series of defeats at the hands of the large Boer army, whose marksmanship and fieldcraft made up for its lack of training. The low point of the war was 'Black Week', when the Boers won battle after battle and drove the British forces to take refuge in fortified towns like

Mafeking, which held out under the command of Robert Baden-Powell, the founder of the Boy Scouts.

More troops were shipped out; a new commander, Lord Roberts, took over from Redvers (unkindly nicknamed 'Reverse') Buller; the sieges were lifted; and the Boers were defeated in several battles. The mood in London was jubilant: when news of the relief of Mafeking came through, crowds went wild with excitement.

The Boer commandoes (a word which owes its origin to this war) now started a guerrilla campaign, which proved extremely difficult to counter. The British response was to conduct huge sweeps across Boer territory, burning farms and putting Boer prisoners, including women and children, into concentration camps (another word coined here), where more than 20,000 of them died of disease. This tactic eventually won the war, but won the British government few friends. There was an international outcry at Britain's treatment of a small nation. Opinion at home was sharply divided: liberals were often pro-Boer, but others thought the Boers needed to be taught a lesson. As the war dragged on and the expense, casualties and cruelties became apparent, more people began to ask awkward questions: could the empire be a force for good if it engaged in 'methods of barbarism'?

1901 Queen Victoria died (her grandson the German Kaiser Wilhelm came to England for her final days) and was succeeded by her sixty-year-old son, Edward VII. Edward was stout, bearded, cigar-smoking and fond of good living: horse-racing, yachting and gambling were his pastimes, and he was also very keen on the ladies.

1902 Britain signed an alliance with Japan, a growing economic and naval power, thus bringing to an end the period of 'Splendid Isolation' (no commitments to another major power) which had lasted for most of the previous century.

1903

The Suffragette Movement Founded

Emmeline Pankhurst founded the Women's Social and Political Union, better known as the suffragettes, to campaign for votes for women. 'Deeds not words', was their motto, and they were not afraid to use violence, including arson, vandalism and personal attacks on leading politicians. Their most spectacular deed came in 1913, when Emily Davison threw herself in front of the king's horse in the Derby and was killed.

The government refused to listen to their cause; when suffragettes in prison went on hunger strike they were force-fed, released to regain their strength and then rearrested under the so-called Cat and Mouse Act. However, the suffragettes' campaign made little impression on the government or on many sectors of public opinion. Newspaper cartoons poked fun at feminist aspirations and debates in Parliament produced hostile or facetious comments. In 1912 the Labour

Party announced its support for votes for women, but it had only 40 MPs.

1904 Britain and France signed the 'Entente Cordiale', not so much a military treaty, more an expression of friendship or a sentimental reconciliation, although both sides realized that it was in their interests to bury their differences and unite against the growing threat of German militarism. King Edward had paved the way for the agreement by his splendid and successful state visit to Paris, the world capital of pleasure and therefore a city close to his heart.

1906 The Liberals won a landslide general election victory against a Conservative Party tarnished by the Boer War and disunited over economic policy. Labour made a real impression for the first time, winning 29 seats. The Liberal government went on to introduce a number of groundbreaking social reforms, such as old age pensions, protection for children and health, and unemployment insurance, thus laying the foundations for the future welfare state.

1907 Britain signed an Entente with Russia. This was even more surprising than the Entente with France, because Russia had been the bogeyman of the British for half a century. Thus the triple Entente – Britain, France, Russia – was born, which went on to be the basis of one side in the First World War.

1909 'We want eight, and we won't wait' was the slogan coined by a Tory MP for the Navy League and others who wanted Britain to build eight Dreadnought battleships in order to stay ahead of Germany in the 'naval race'.

1910 Lloyd George, the Liberal Chancellor, introduced the 'People's Budget', with taxes aimed at the rich such as inheritance tax on landed estates and supertax on high incomes. The outraged House of Lords threw out the Budget and provoked a constitutional crisis which ended with the powers of the Lords being curbed for good (in the 1911 Parliament Act). This may have been Lloyd George's intention all along – he memorably described the House of Lords (all hereditary peers at the time) as 'five hundred men chosen at random from amongst the unemployed'.

1911 Salaries for MPs were introduced, thus making it easier for working men to enter Parliament.

1914–18

The First World War

In the first two months of the war no fewer than 750,000 Britons volunteered for the armed forces. Kitchener's posters ('your country needs you') suggested that no young man of spirit could afford to miss the fun. Patriotic ladies handed white feathers to men of military age who were not in uniform. The suffragettes announced the suspension of their campaign while the war lasted. Even many Catholic Irishmen signed up to fight. Britain, like most of the combatants, was overcome by an orgy of patriotism and war fever. When the assassination of Archduke Franz Ferdinand triggered the deadly system of European alliances into action, Britain had no firm commitment to any of the powers involved. Officially, the reason for Britain's declaration of war on Germany was that the German army had attacked France through 'gallant little Belgium', which Britain was bound to protect under a treaty dating back to the 1830s. But what would Britain have done if France had attacked Germany through Belgium –

declared war on France? In fact, Britain went to war to stop Germany dominating the Continent, because the Kaiser's next move might well have been to start whittling away at the British empire. Compared with the vast conscript armies of the other powers, Britain's professional army in 1914 was tiny, but the British Expeditionary Force (BEF) was highly trained and well prepared for the job of crossing the Channel and linking up with the French. At the battle of Mons the rifle fire of the BEF was so rapid that the Germans believed they were facing machine guns (of which the British in fact had very few). The Kaiser had spoken of Britain's 'contemptible little army', but it fought heroically and suffered huge losses to slow down the German advance and help save France from an early defeat.

The trenches

'Fighting machine gun bullets with the breasts of young men.' This was Winston Churchill's description of the tactics used at the battle of the Somme in 1916. Almost 20,000 men were killed on the first day at the Somme – the worst casualties ever suffered in a day by the British Army – and they were mostly the volunteers from 1914, 'Kitchener's army', the young men who had answered their country's call when war broke out. The mud, blood and horror of the war in the trenches have been well documented by diarists, poets, historians and film makers, and the conventional view is of 'lions led by donkeys': in other words, an army of brave men brutalized by the war and sent 'over the top' into the meat-grinder of senseless frontal assaults by generals who took care to remain well behind the front line in comfortable accommodation. Of course, this is an over-simplification: many men were damaged psycho-logically as well as physically by the experience of the trenches, but others relished the comradeship and excitement of war. At the dreadful battle of Passchendaele in 1917, where men literally drowned in the mud, General Haig did persist with tactics which the battle of the Somme had shown to be fruitless; but Haig's critics have had great difficulty in suggesting alternative tactics, except with the luxury of hindsight, and his commitment to 'attrition' did help to wear down the enemy.

The Home Front

Just as this was the first mechanized war – with tanks, lorries, armoured cars and planes – so it was the first 'total war', a war which affected the daily lives of civil-ians in all sorts of ways. Public information was strictly controlled – the first day on the Somme was presented as a great victory, for example – and propaganda was crude if effective: most people happily swallowed horror stories about German barbarism, such as the factory behind the lines which allegedly processed corpses into fats, oils and pigfood. Conscription was introduced in 1916, and although it was possible for conscientious objectors ('conchies') to do war work which did not involve fighting, many ended up in prison. Food rationing was enforced because the German U-boats sank so many merchant ships bringing supplies across the Atlantic. Women had to take over the jobs of men away at the front, labouring on farms, running essential public services and working as 'munitionettes' in arms factories. The government nationalized railways, shipping and other industries and banned strikes. The police were given extraordinary powers to round up enemy aliens and hold suspects without trial. In fact, the war meant an enormous invasion of personal freedom for almost everyone in Britain.

The worldwide war

The trenches of the Western Front provide the iconic image of the Great War, and this is where the war was finally won and lost, but British troops also saw action in Africa and the Middle East. In 1915 a badly planned and hastily put together expedition was sent to Gallipoli to attack Germany's ally Turkey and open up the Black Sea for the benefit of Russia. The landings on the Gallipoli peninsula were a shambles and the attackers got pinned down into trench warfare by the Turks, who held the high ground. Thousands of men died of exposure and disease, and the only successful thing about the campaign was the withdrawal, which was conducted rapidly and without serious casualties. Many of the troops at Gallipoli were Australians and New Zealanders (ANZAC) – in fact, troops from the empire, including India (the largest of the colonial armies), made up about a quarter of total British forces, and of all the countries involved in the war little New

Zealand lost proportionately the most men. The other vital theatre for Britain was the war at sea. The U-boats were finally defeated by the convoy system and by improved technology such as depth charges and tracking from the air. The German High Seas Fleet went out of port in force only once and met the British Grand Fleet at the battle of Jutland in 1916. German gunnery proved to be superior and the British lost fourteen ships to the Germans' eleven, but the German fleet retreated into port in the face of superior British numbers and did not re-emerge for the rest of the war. The Royal Navy was therefore able to continue its blockade of German ports, starving the country of vital food and raw materials and contributing greatly to the final victory.

The end of the war

The war which was supposed to be 'over by Christmas' dragged on for four years. Patriotic enthusiasm gave way to war weariness as the casualty lists lengthened and rationing began to bite. In 1917 Russia dropped out after the communist revolution, but the USA came in when U-boats started sinking American shipping. In early 1918 Germany mounted one last big offensive which pushed the Allies back all along the Front and got dangerously close to Paris, but it could not sustain its advance in the face of the Americans, who were now arriving in large numbers. In August British troops, led by nearly 500 tanks, started the counter-offensive which drove the German forces back, and on 11 November

(Armistice Day) the Germans surrendered. Over a period of four years six million Britons had volunteered or been called up, three-quarters of a million had lost their lives and many hundreds of thousands suffered the physical or mental scars of war.

1916 The Easter Rising. At Easter a group of extremist Irish Nationalists seized the General Post Office and other key buildings in Dublin and proclaimed Ireland an independent republic. The Easter Rising was put down by the British Army after a week of fighting in which nearly 500 people were killed. The government treated the rebel leaders as traitors and fifteen were executed. These people were seen in Ireland as martyrs, and although most Irish people did not originally support the Rising, a reaction against Britain set in. Sinn Fein ('ourselves alone'), the party which supported complete independence for Ireland, exploited this mood and in the 1918 general election won three-quarters of Irish seats.

1918 The Representation of the People Act gave the vote to all men over 21 and to most women over 30 (women under 30 – 'flappers' as they came to be called – were thought to be too irresponsible or frivolous). The subsequent general election was won by a Conservative/Liberal coalition under the leadership of Lloyd George, who as prime minister of a coalition government since 1916, was admired as the 'man who won the war'. Some Liberals refused to join the coalition (this fatal split was the beginning of the end for the Liberals as a serious force). Labour won over 60 seats and emerged as a fully independent party.

1919 The Amritsar Massacre. British troops under the command of General Dyer opened fire on a crowd in a garden called Jalianwala Bagh in the Indian city of Amritsar in the Punjab, killing about 400 people. There had earlier been a riot in which two Britons had been killed, but the crowd was taking part in a peaceful demonstration when British troops opened fire without warning and continued firing for ten minutes. Dyer's 'firm' action was supported by the local British authorities and although he was relieved of his command and sent home, admirers presented him with money and a sword inscribed 'Saviour of the Punjab'. The Amritsar Massacre turned many Indians against British rule, and Gandhi's campaign for independence gained momentum.

1921 Foundation of the Irish Free State. Southern Ireland became the Irish Free State, with effective independence but still under the British Crown and part of the empire, much like Australia or Canada. Northern Ireland remained part of the United Kingdom. The Anglo-Irish treaty which divided Ireland, and which had been skilfully negotiated by Lloyd George with the leaders of both sides, was the only possible way to end the vicious war between the Irish Republican Army (IRA) and British troops, supported by police and

'Black and Tan' volunteers. A civil war then erupted in the South between pro- and anti-treaty factions within the IRA, which the Regulars (supporting the treaty) won. In 1937 the Irish Free State was renamed Eire and in 1949 the last formal link with Britain was cut and Eire became a completely independent republic.

1922 The Fall of Lloyd George. The Conservative majority in the coalition government ditched its Liberal Prime Minister Lloyd George, whose increasingly autocratic style, notorious womanizing and involvement in the sale of peerages ('Lloyd George knew my father') were proving an embarrassment. At the subsequent general election Liberal support was split between Lloyd George and the previous leader Asquith, and the party's share of the vote slumped. The Conservatives won easily and Labour became the official opposition with nearly 150 seats.

1924 Ramsay MacDonald became the first Labour prime minister. 'Today 23 years ago dear Grandmama died. I wonder what she would have thought of a Labour government!' This was from George V's diary on the day that he invited Ramsay MacDonald to become prime minister. MacDonald and his Labour colleagues lacked experience in government and many came from very humble backgrounds (MacDonald himself was the illegitimate son of a serving maid). Conservative Britain was appalled – Winston Churchill called it 'a serious national misfortune' – and although the minority Labour government proved to be very moderate it survived for less than a year. The Zinoviev letter – a faked letter from the Russian government to British communists and containing directions for starting a revolution in Britain – was used by the *Daily Mail* to smear Labour ('Moscow Orders to Our Reds') and the Conservatives won a landslide election victory.

1926

The General Strike

'Not a penny off the pay, not a minute on the day.' With these defiant words a strike by the coal miners (then over one million strong) escalated into a call by the Trades Union Congress (TUC) for a general strike of all workers. Another two million people in transport, the building trade and many other industries responded to this call for working-class solidarity and came out on strike.

Stanley Baldwin's Conservative government treated the strike as an attempt to overawe legal authority, the government's official newssheet calling it 'a direct challenge to ordered government'. But this was not the intention of the TUC: it could not afford a long strike, it did not believe in revolutionary violence and its main aim was simply to achieve a deal for the miners. Middle-class volunteers flocked to drive buses and keep other public services running and the strikers jeered them, but there was almost no violence. In the event, the General Strike – the only one in British history –

lasted for just nine days before the TUC called it off. The government subsequently restricted the powers of trade unions, although employers did become warier of provoking strikes by cutting wages. The unfortunate miners stayed out on strike for months before being starved back to work. Left-wingers have seen the strike as being deliberately provoked by the government and its outcome as a sell-out of ordinary workers by the union leaders. Those on the right have seen it as a healthy defeat for dangerously militant trade unionism. Perhaps it is best seen as an expression of typically British moderation and compromise: a confrontation which in a more excitable nation could have developed into bloodshed and revolution was conducted in an orderly manner by both sides and ended without serious recriminations.

1927 The British Broadcasting Corporation was granted a Royal Charter and exclusive rights to radio broadcasting. The BBC's tradition of independent but publicly funded broadcasting was established, and John (later Lord) Reith, the first Director General, defined the BBC's mission as to 'inform, educate and entertain'. For Reith, a serious-minded Scotsman, entertainment was definitely last on the list.

1928 Women over 21 got the vote, so political equality between the sexes was achieved at last.

1931 The Statute of Westminster gave complete self-government to the dominions within the British empire or 'Commonwealth' as it was beginning to be called. This applied to Australia, New Zealand, Canada, Newfoundland and South Africa, but not to India, where resistance to British rule continued.

1932 Oswald Mosley founded the British Union of Fascists, in imitation of Mussolini who was already dictator of Italy and Hitler who was to take power in Germany in 1933.

1933 'This house will under no circumstances fight for king and country'. By a vote of almost two to one the Oxford University Union passed this motion, which was typical of the national mood of the time: fearful of a repeat of the horrors of the Great War and in favour of solving international problems by negotiation through the League of Nations.

1935 Britain and Germany signed a naval agreement which allowed Hitler to rebuild the German navy (strictly forbidden by the treaty which ended the Great War). The deal was that Germany could build warships up to a total of one-third the size of the Royal Navy. This was an early sign of British gullibility when faced with Hitler (he soon broke the agreement) as well as the beginning of the fatal policy of appeasement (making concessions to Hitler in the belief that this would keep the peace) – to say nothing of it being a slap in the face to Britain's former ally France, which was not consulted and which had far more reason to fear Germany.

1936 Edward VIII abdicated. 'I have found it impossible to carry the heavy burden of responsibility and to discharge my duties as king as I would wish to do without the help and support of the woman I love.' With these words Edward VIII became the only monarch in British history to abdicate voluntarily, having reigned for less than a year. His desire to marry Wallis Simpson, a twice-divorced American with a shady past, was unacceptable to the British establishment and the Commonwealth. The throne passed to his brother, George VI. Then as now a royal scandal provided plenty of gossip and fun: a popular carol at Christmas 1936 ran 'Hark the herald angels sing, Mrs Simpson's got our king!'

1938

The Munich Crisis

At a conference in Munich held in September 1938 it was agreed by Britain, France and Italy that Germany could take possession of the Sudetenland, the area of Czechoslovakia where many ethnic Germans lived and which Hitler had been threatening to invade and conquer. On his return from Munich the prime minister, Neville Chamberlain, called the agreement 'peace with honour . . . peace in our time' and waved the 'piece of paper' with Hitler's signature on it which he said meant that Britain and Germany would never go to war again. Most people cheered Chamberlain, but a few pointed out that the Czechs had been betrayed (they were not even present at the conference which dismembered their country) and that Munich amounted to surrender to Hitler's aggression. Winston Churchill, who had consistently opposed appeasement and advocated re-arming Britain, called it 'a total unmitigated defeat'. Munich was the culmination of the policy of appeasement towards Hitler; he had already been allowed to build up Germany's armed forces, station troops on the French border and annex Austria. Now he was convinced that Britain and France lacked the backbone to face up to him whatever he did. Historians have disputed whether there was a real alternative to appeasement – there would have been huge practical difficulties in actually helping the Czechs resist Hitler, and appeasement did buy time for Britain to build up the RAF – but Munich still leaves a bad taste in the mouth. Chamberlain's description of 'a quarrel in a faraway country between people of whom we know nothing' seems like little more than a refusal to face up to responsibility.

1939–45

The Second World War

War breaks out

When Hitler invaded and took over the whole of Czechoslovakia in early 1939 it was clear that the policy of appeasement was a total failure. Britain now gave a guarantee to Poland – Hitler's next target – that it would come to its aid if attacked. When Germany crossed Poland's borders in September, Britain declared war. In fact, there was nothing Britain could do to assist the Poles – especially since a half-hearted attempt to sign a treaty with Russia had failed and the Russians were now allies of Germany – and Poland was soon conquered and absorbed by Germany and Russia. Seven months of 'Phoney War' followed, during which the only action was at sea. Britain spent this time preparing gas masks, ration cards, blackout regulations, air raid shelters and call-up papers as well as sending an expeditionary force of nearly 200,000 men to France. Chamberlain confidently announced that Hitler had 'missed the bus'. Four days later German forces swept into Denmark and Norway. Britain sent a force to help the Norwegians but it achieved nothing and had to be evacuated. Chamberlain was now losing the support even of his own party – a backbencher used the words of Oliver Cromwell to demand, 'In the name of God, go!' – and in May 1940 Chamberlain resigned and the king sent for Winston Churchill to form a new government. Churchill, in the first of the wartime speeches which were to go down in history, told Parliament that all he had to offer was 'blood, toil, tears and sweat'.

1940–41 Britain alone

The very day that Churchill took office the German armies made their move in the west, advancing quickly through Belgium and Holland and breaking into France. The German *blitzkrieg* was so rapid and so effective that the BEF and much of the French army were cut off in northern France. With France crumbling to defeat (the country surrendered in just six weeks) there was no choice for the British but to retreat to the coast. At Dunkirk defeat was turned into a kind of victory by the successful evacuation in just a week of almost the entire British army, although it left behind nearly all its weapons and equipment. With France defeated and other friendly states already overrun, Britain now stood alone. As Churchill said, 'the battle of France is over. The battle of Britain is about to begin'. Hitler made plans to invade, but he had to achieve command of the air in order to have any hope of overcoming the Royal Navy in the Channel, and in the

Battle of Britain (1940) in the summer skies over southern England the RAF defeated the Luftwaffe. 'Never in the field of human conflict,' said Churchill, 'was so much owed by so many to so few.' But one reason for the RAF's victory was that the Germans had switched their efforts from attacking military targets to bombing cities. This was the Blitz, and it was to last at high intensity until the middle of 1941. The 'Britain can take it' spirit of the Blitz and the heroics of the Battle of Britain were good for morale, as was Churchill's reassurance that this was Britain's 'finest hour', but a more practically useful contribution came from across the Atlantic. Churchill pleaded to the Americans, 'Give us the tools and we will finish the job,' and their response was the Lend-Lease scheme, which made American loans and war material available to Britain. The only actual victories to celebrate were in North Africa, where British armies thoroughly defeated the Italians – although German reinforcements under Rommel soon pushed the British out of the conquered territory.

1941–5 Winning the war

In June 1941 Hitler attacked Russia. Instantly, Britain had a new ally and the Blitz slackened as German bombers were moved to the Eastern Front. In December 1941 Japan attacked the American fleet at Pearl Harbour, Germany declared war on the USA and Britain declared war on Japan. Instead of standing alone, Britain was now a partner in a triple alliance, and when

Churchill heard the news of Pearl Harbour he said with relief, 'So we have won after all'. Of course, there were still defeats and hardships to come: the loss of Tobruk in North Africa, the surrender of Singapore and the Dieppe raid were all disasters for British arms; rationing, shortages and restrictions were all causes for complaint at home; and the German V1 flying bombs and V2 rockets hit London hard in 1944, just when the war appeared to be coming to an end. But Montgomery's victory over Rommel at El Alamein in November 1942 marked the turn of the tide for Britain; as Churchill rightly judged, 'This is not the end. It is not even the beginning of the end. But it is, perhaps, the end of the beginning.' Having stood alone for a vital year, it was not easy for Britain to accept that it was now over-shadowed militarily by its two mighty allies. Certainly Britain provided the springboard for the D-day invasion and British forces played an important role in the final stages of the war in Europe, as well as a smaller part in the defeat of Japan. But the fact remained that Germany had been defeated mainly by Russia on the Eastern Front and Japan's defeat was mostly down to America, especially to the atomic bomb. At the wartime and postwar conferences Churchill appeared to be the equal of Stalin and Roosevelt, but British forces were much weaker than those of either of their allies and the war had almost bankrupted Britain. Although Britain was a victor, an occupying power in Germany, a permanent member of the Security Council of the new United Nations and still the possessor of an enormous empire, was it still a genuine world power?

1945 Labour won a landslide victory in the general election. Halfway through the Potsdam conference of Allied leaders, and to the astonishment of Stalin, whose grasp of the democratic process was somewhat shaky, Churchill's Conservative Party lost the post-VE Day general election to Labour by a huge margin. Voters respected Churchill as a war leader but believed that Attlee's Labour Party would be better able to reconstruct the country and carry out necessary welfare reforms.

1946

The Foundation of the
Welfare State

The National Health Act and the National Insurance
Act became law. These were the centrepieces of the
Labour government's programme to put into practice
the recommendations of the 1942 Beveridge Report.
The report had proposed that after the war the state
should look after its citizens 'from the cradle to the
grave' and declared that there were five giants to be
overcome in the creation of a better society: Want,
Ignorance, Disease, Squalor and Idleness.

The Education Act of 1944 had already tackled
Ignorance, with the creation of free secondary education for all in secondary modern and grammar schools.
Later, family allowances, increased pensions and a
revised and more comprehensive system of benefits
were all introduced. Over a million council houses
were built, unemployment fell and key industries such
as transport and mining were nationalized. But despite

the creation of the welfare state, rationing and shortages continued in the postwar years.

1947 India was granted independence. India was costing Britain money, self-rule had been promised, Labour was committed to independence and the Quit India movement was gaining massive support. Lord Mountbatten was sent to India as its last Viceroy and was forced to propose partition of the country into a mostly Muslim Pakistan and a mostly Hindu India. In the violence which followed nearly a million people died and many others became refugees.

1948 The National Health Service came into being, offering for the first time free health care to all.

1952 King George VI died and Princess Elizabeth became Queen Elizabeth II. Her coronation the following year boosted the sale of TV sets, and the accession of a young and attractive queen, together with the first ascent of Everest by Hillary and Tenzing and the first four-minute mile by Roger Bannister (1954), led to much optimistic talk about the dawning of a 'new Elizabethan Age'.

1954 Rationing ended and the economy started to pick up, so much so that Conservative Prime Minister Harold Macmillan could declare to the British people in 1957, 'You've never had it so good'.

1956

The Suez Crisis

Egypt, although officially independent, had long been under British influence and in the early 1950s about 40,000 British troops were still based there to protect Britain's interests in the Middle East – mostly oil and the important trade routes through the Anglo-French-owned Suez Canal. When the Egyptian President Nasser made it clear that he wanted Britain out and nationalized the canal, the response of Prime Minister Anthony Eden was to treat Nasser as a sort of born-again Hitler who must not be appeased and then to hatch a cunning plan with the French and the Israelis. Israel was to attack Egypt so that Britain and France would have the perfect excuse to send troops into the canal zone to 'restore order'. The plan was duly put into action, but within days Britain had to order a cease-fire and then withdraw its troops because the USA, who had not been consulted in advance, was appalled by this threat to the stability of the Middle East and led a vote in the UN condemning Britain's action. At the same time the USA put pressure on British gold and dollar reserves, and all the Commonwealth countries except Australia came out against Britain. The very public humiliation involved in Britain's climbdown was a signal that it was no longer a world power. It also marked the beginning of the end of the British empire and a period of uncertainty about Britain's international position during which it was said (1962) by former US Secretary of State Dean Acheson that, 'Great Britain has lost an empire but not yet found a role'.

1960 Macmillan's 'wind of change' speech. 'The wind of change is blowing through this continent,' said Prime Minister Harold Macmillan in a speech in South Africa, recognizing the fact that Britain was dismantling its African empire. The royal family was kept busy travelling to flag-lowering ceremonies, since most of Britain's African colonies gained their independence in the late 1950s and early '60s, as did other British possessions such as Malaya. By the early 1970s the only remaining colonies were small islands and the only one of any significance was Hong Kong.

1961 *Beyond the Fringe* **was staged in London**. Its satirical attacks on figures of authority, including the prime minister, underlined a new spirit of rebellion and a rejection of traditional morality, which had already been seen in the novels and plays of the 'angry young men' and in the publication (1960) of *Lady Chatterley's Lover* after its unsuccessful prosecution for obscenity.

The 'satire boom' was represented on TV by *That Was the Week that Was* (from 1962), which coincided with the Profumo scandal, a powerful mix of sex, snobbery and espionage that provided the programme with the perfect excuse to poke fun at the government.

1962 The Beatles released *Love Me Do*, their first hit. The word 'teenager' had already been coined in the 1950s, but it was in the 1960s that a distinctive youth culture took shape, based on fashion and music but branching out later in the decade into 'alternative lifestyles' and the politics of protest.

1963 General de Gaulle said 'Non' to Britain's application to join the European Common Market. Britain had not bothered to apply for membership when the Common Market was set up in 1957, and de Gaulle doubted Britain's commitment to Europe and suspected that its ties to the Commonwealth and the USA were more important to Britain.

1966 England won the World Cup and *Time* magazine declared London to be 'the swinging city'. The Union Jack became a fashion accessory, but when it was printed on T-shirts as part of the 'I'm Backing Britain' campaign (1968) to encourage people to buy British goods, it was unfortunately revealed that the T-shirts had been made in Portugal.

1968 The 'Troubles' began in Northern Ireland when a Catholic Civil Rights march in (London)derry ended in a riot. Over the next three decades political violence and terrorism caused several thousand deaths in Northern Ireland and more than a hundred on the British mainland.

1973 Britain joined the European Community after Prime Minister Edward Heath convinced the French that the British would become good Europeans. British commitment to Europe was tested in 1975 when the Labour government of Harold Wilson held a referendum on whether to stay in Europe. The result was a 67 per cent 'yes' vote – convincing, but hardly overwhelming.

1975 The first North Sea oil came ashore. This was a bright moment in the generally gloomy economic climate of the 1970s. The term 'stagflation' was coined to describe a mixture of stagnation and inflation, and there was much talk of 'the British disease' – the inability of management and workers to cooperate and the consequent disruption of industry by widespread strikes. Particularly low points were the three-day week caused by the miners' strike of the early 1970s and the 'winter of discontent' in 1978/9, when many private- and public-sector workers went on strike.

1979 Margaret Thatcher became Britain's first woman prime minister. Taking advantage of Labour's economic troubles and a general feeling that the trade unions had got out of control, Mrs Thatcher promised to curb union power and reduce inflation, taxation and public spending; she also stressed her firm attitude to law and order, defence and immigration. Once in power, she dominated her cabinet and refused to shift from the policies she was elected on.

1982 Argentina invaded the Falkland Islands, a British colony in the South Atlantic. A British naval task force was sent to recover the islands, which they rapidly did but at the cost of 255 men killed and six ships lost (Argentine casualties were much higher). Some critics claimed that Britain should have seen the conflict coming and reacted sooner. Others (but very few) condemned the campaign as the last spasm of an outdated imperialism. But most people were delighted that the British lion had shown it still had some teeth. Mrs Thatcher's profile was raised at home and abroad ('the iron lady') and the popularity of her government was confirmed at the 1983 election with a large majority.

1984

Foundation of the World Wide Web

The Internet had many inventors, but one man can lay claim to formulating the codes and protocols that set the foundations of the World Wide Web. The first attempts to link a network of computers had been developed throughout the 1960s and '70s as part of a mixed academic and military operation. The first network was set up at the University of California, Los Angeles, in 1969. By the 1980s many of the major institutions had become linked to this network but there was no easy way to navigate the system.

In 1984, Tim Berners Lee, a British freelance computer programmer, was working at CERN, the European Organization for Nuclear Research in Switzerland. CERN had one of the most sophisticated computer systems in the world and was a central part of the developing internet network. Berners Lee saw a way of combining the internet with a programme of hyper-text, which allowed information to be linked.

He then created a whole architecture to organize this protocol, which he called the World Wide Web. The new hypertext transfer protocol (http) allowed easier use and navigation.

Berners Lee gave his invention away, refusing to patent it and allowing anyone who wished access to the internet to have it. By 1990, most of the internet had adopted this method. Indeed, every website that starts with 'www' has Berners Lee to thank. But as the inventor once noted in an interview, 'Even the clearest, cleverest and most comprehensive website cannot hope to equal the wealth of information contained in a good reference book. The internet is most definitely not a substitute for a well-stocked public library.'

Monarchs since the Norman Conquest in 1066 showing the dates of their reigns

House of Normandy

1066–1087	William I
1087–1100	William II
1100–1135	Henry I
1135–1154	Stephen

House of Plantagenet

1154–1189	Henry II
1189–1199	Richard I
1199–1216	John
1216–1272	Henry III
1272–1307	Edward I
1307–1327	Edward II
1327–1377	Edward III
1377–1399	Richard II

House of Lancaster

1399–1413	Henry IV
1413–1422	Henry V
1422–1461	Henry VI

House of York

1461–1483	Edward IV
1483	Edward V
1483–1485	Richard III

House of Tudor

1485–1509	Henry VII
1509–1547	Henry VIII
1547–1553	Edward VI
1553–1558	Mary I
1558–1603	Elizabeth I

House of Stuart

1603–1625	James I
1625–1649	Charles I

Interregnum

1649–1653	Commonwealth/ protectorate
1653–1658	Protectorate of Oliver Cromwell
1658–1659	Protectorate of Richard Cromwell

House of Stuart restored

1660–1685	Charles II
1685–1688	James II
1689–1694	William and Mary (jointly)

House of Orange

1694–1702	William III (sole ruler)
1702–1714	Anne

House of Hanover

1714–1727	George I
1727–1760	George II
1760–1820	George III
1820–1830	George IV
1830–1837	William IV
1837–1901	Victoria

House of Saxe-Coburg

1901–1910	Edward VII

House of Windsor

1910–1936	George V (a Saxe-Coburg until 1917)
1936	Edward VIII
1936–1952	George VI
1952–	Elizabeth II

Willy, Willy, Harry, Ste[ve],
Harry, Dick, John, Harry 3.
1 2 3 Neds, Richard 2
Henry 4 5 6, then who?
Edward 4 5, Dick the Bad,
Harrys twain, then Ned the Lad.
Mary, Lizzie, James the Vain,
Charlie, Charlie, James again.
William & Mary, Anna Gloria,
4 Georges, William and Victoria.
Edward, George, the same again,
Elizabeth 2 and long may she reign!